There's never been a book on American whiskeys like this one!

"These guys did one hell of a wonderful job. *The Book of Classic American Whiskeys* tells the whole story, the way it truly is, with a lot of interesting details. I've never read a better book on whiskey."

> —F. BOOKER NOE, JR.
> Grandson of Jim Beam
> Master Distiller Emeritus
> James B. Beam Distilling Company

"Never before has any publication on American whiskeys included so many brands and taste profiles. *The Book of Classic American Whiskeys* is a very current and up-to-date look at whiskey, but its historical sections also make for captivating reading. It presents the real story behind one of America's great, though somewhat overlooked, industries."

> —CHRIS MORRIS
> Bourbon Heritage Manager
> United Distillers Manufacturing

"Mark Waymack and Jim Harris have managed to synthesize in one book what it took me over 40 years to learn as Master Distiller for Wild Turkey Bourbon. *The Book of Classic American Whiskeys* is, by far, the most authoritative, exhaustive work on the Bourbon and whiskey industry available today."

> —JIMMY RUSSELL
> Master Distiller
> Wild Turkey

THE BOOK OF
—Classic—
American
WHISKEYS

Mark H. Waymack
and
James F. Harris

OPEN  COURT

Chicago and La Salle, Illinois

©1995 by Open Court Publishing Company

First printing 1995

Printed and bound in the United States of America.

Library of Congress Cataloging-in-Publication Data

Waymack, Mark H.
    The book of classic American whiskeys / Mark H. Waymack and James
  F. Harris.
       p. cm.
    Includes bibliographical references and index.
    ISBN 0-8126-9305-1. — ISBN 0-8126-9306-X (pbk.)
    1. Whiskey—United States. I. Harris, James F. (James Franklin).
 1941– . II. Title
 TP605.W39   1995
 641.2'52'0973—dc   2095-16647
                                            CIP

Abusus non tollit usum

(Abuse is not evidence against proper use)

Note to the Updated
Second Printing

The enthusiastic reception of this book upon its release has led Open Court to produce a second printing just two months after the first. While this printing is not strictly a new *edition*, we have been allowed the opportunity to make some minor corrections and also some significant changes throughout the text.

Among notable developments, after serving for decades as Master Distiller at the Seagram's Four Roses Distillery, Ova Haney has retired. And after many years of not offering its Bourbon in the U.S., Seagram's introduces a single-barrel version of Four Roses in January 1996. (These items and an accompanying tasting note are found on pages 149–150.) We have also included two new single-barrel Bourbons from Heaven Hill.

Finally, as we pointed out below, some distilleries hold dozens, even hundreds, of labels, and there is a constant trafficking of these labels among distilleries. To attempt to keep up with all of those changing labels would be doomed to futility, as well as being an inappropriate ambition for a book of enduring value. As we explain in the Preface, we have concentrated on the *classic* whiskeys. These labels are held very closely by their owners. Hence, while several dozens of labels changed hands in 1995 (so that any tasting notes on these labels would have become obsolete, as the contents of the bottle changed), only one label that we discuss is affected: Kentucky Tavern moves from United Distillers to Barton Distilling. For some sense of what Kentucky Tavern will taste like, consult our note on Very Old Barton, on page 93.

M.H.W. and J.F.H.
October 1995

Contents

Preface

When our editor at Open Court, David Ramsay Steele, first suggested writing a book on American whiskeys following the publication of our earlier book, *Single-Malt Whiskies of Scotland,* we were skeptical and reluctant. First, we thought, surely there must already be such a book, or even several of them. Secondly, we were not sure how attractive to a general audience such a book would be. We soon discovered, to our surprise, that although there have been a few books done on Bourbon Whiskey, these are all very limited and dated, and most of them are now out of print. In any case, as far as we can determine, no one has ever written a book about American whiskeys which is anything like this one. What really made up our minds, however, was our discovery of just how unexpectedly fascinating and rewarding the whole subject of American whiskey is.

Readers will come to this book with different interests. You *can,* if you feel you absolutely *must,* follow and understand any one of the chapters without having read any of the others. Let us therefore outline here the topics we cover in the different chapters.

More than half of the book (Chapters 3 and 4) provides a detailed account, distillery by distillery, of the best brands of whiskey produced in the United States today. The focus here is on *the best labels now available,* though in passing we do say much about whiskey in general and about great labels of the past, now out of commission. We present 'tasting notes' describing and evaluating the character of these outstanding drinks, we describe peculiarities of their manufacture which may account for their individual characters, we give something of the histories of the distilleries, and in doing so we dispel some misconceptions and dubious legends. The reader will also learn something here of the intriguing personalities, past and present, who have helped to make the American whiskey industry such a wondrous benefit to the arts and diversions of humankind.

All of the truly great American whiskeys now marketed fall into one of two categories: they are Kentucky Bourbons (the subject of Chapter 3) or Tennessee Whiskeys (the topic of Chapter 4). Anyone who reads these two chapters will possess a complete and accurate understanding of exactly what defines these two categories of spirits—historically, legally, technologically, and even gustatorily, to the extent that this last can be absorbed without actually imbibing the stuff. These chapters also include descriptions of the distillery premises themselves, and advice for those growing numbers of people all over the world who desire to visit them.

Before those two chapters we have placed a fairly long chapter on the history of American whiskey (Chapter 1) and a fairly short chapter on the process by which whiskey is manufactured (Chapter 2).

Chapter 1 will come as a revelation to many readers. The history of the United States of America *is* the history of American whiskey. If you think that's a reckless exaggeration, then you need to read Chapter 1 and think again. We believe you will agree that if it is indeed something of an exaggeration, it is an instructive and far from reckless one.

Chapter 2 can be skipped on a first reading. It describes the way in which American whiskey is made. We do urge you to read it eventually if not straight away: it is helpful background and elucidation for much else in the book.

One of the qualities that distinguishes the best American whiskeys from the best single-malt Scotches—which it would be a cardinal sin to adulterate with any other substance, even (in most cases) water—is that American whiskeys, being sweeter, do mix well. Our last chapter, Chapter 5, offers practical advice on arranging convivial whiskey tastings in your own home, and gives our pick of the recipes (for cocktails, appetizers, entrees, side dishes, and desserts) which utilize American whiskey.

This is a book about *classic* American whiskeys. Although it is far more comprehensive than any other currently available book on American whiskeys, it is not an encyclopedia. We should briefly mention here three of the topics we do *not* discuss in detail. First, we don't have much to say about rye whiskey. Since the repeal of Prohibition, rye whiskey has steadily dwindled in importance, and is now marginal. Only two or three distilleries continue to produce rye whiskey, and their production runs are infrequent and small. Second, we say little about blended whiskeys. There are hundreds of these labels, their character and subtlety of flavor are definitely well below those of the true Bourbon or Tennessee whiskeys, and we do not regard them as meriting inclusion among 'classic' whiskeys.

Finally, we give scant attention to 'contract whiskey'—whiskey bottled and marketed by one firm which has purchased it from another firm, the actual distiller. Some contract whiskeys are quite fine, but at best they will be no better than whiskey bottled at the distillery which produced it. The provenance of contract whiskeys is not advertised and can be difficult to ascertain. We have chosen to keep our focus upon the people who actually make the whiskey. Our rule has been to discuss at length only the labels of those distilleries who have shown us that they make their own straight Bourbon or Tennessee whiskey, and whose whiskey is of the consistently high quality that merits the appellation 'classic'.

Researching and writing this book have been particularly enjoyable because of the very special people we have met and gotten to know during our trips to Kentucky and Tennessee. We have benefitted enormously from the warm camaraderie we found among the handful of talented men who produce America's finest whiskeys.

We were not sure exactly just how we would be received. Here we were, a couple of college professors, and *philosophers* at that,

wanting to write a book about American whiskey. We were afraid
that people would be suspicious of us and reticent to talk to us. We
suspected that there might be many trade secrets which people didn't
want to share. We played up our Southern heritage (Harris is a
native Tennessean and Waymack is a native Virginian) and our rural roots. The success of *Single-Malt Whiskies of Scotland* earned us
instant respect. We were surprised and pleased at the very cordial,
co-operative, and genuinely friendly reception which we received.

   This is a part of the country where everyone seems to know everyone else. In many cases, these men have known each other since
early childhood. They are lifelong friends and since many of the
families involved are quite large, that means that the members of
the extended families—the aunts and uncles and cousins—also all
know each other.

   It is part of the nature of life in small Southern towns that not
much remains secret for very long. For example, much to our amuse-
ment and astonishment, as we made our first research tour through
Kentucky everyone we visited seemed to know where we had already been and where we were next headed. The grapevine works
well indeed. Only later did we learn that people were telephoning
each other to chat about 'the two guys writing the book.'

   This is a group of people who are all very proud of what they
do, and they have a marvellous zest for life. Stories of ancestors,
accounts of great adventures and fond reminiscences along with
just plain 'tall tales' were sprinkled throughout nearly every conversation.

   These men like to enjoy life and, in the finest of the 'good old
boy' tradition are not above having their fun at each other's expense
(or even at their own). Our first encounter with Jimmy Russell,
Master Distiller at Wild Turkey and Booker Noe, former Master
Distiller at Jim Beam and Jim Beam's grandson, serves as a good
example of the kind of relationship we are trying to describe. These
two men are each enormously important, highly respected, much
beloved figures in the whiskey industry. When we interviewed Jimmy
Russell, we told him that we were later supposed to see Booker. He
said with a wry grin, "Well, give that old S.O.B. a good 'cussing out,'
and then tell him that I said so!" When we went to have lunch with

Booker at his home the next day and were introduced, Booker said, "Well, I hear that you boys are writing a book." Harris shook hands with Booker and said, "Well, I've heard a lot about you too." "Oh, what's that?" Booker asked. "Well, I've been told that you don't know jack-s . . . about making Bourbon," Harris said. Booker huffed and puffed and pretended to be offended and let out with a loud and slow, "Naaawww, who told you that? You must have been talking to Jimmy Russell up at Lawrenceburg!" And we all had a good laugh. Only upon our second visit to Kentucky did we learn that Jerry Dalton, of Barton Brands, (with whom we had an interesting conversation about Taoism and reading the *Tao Te Ching*) had warned Booker of our intent before our arrival at his house. So, in the end, the laugh was on us, but we had a good laugh nonetheless and now have one more story to tell.

Despite the competitive nature of the whiskey-making business there is a great degree of co-operation among the people actually responsible for making the whiskey. As Jimmy Russell, of Wild Turkey, put it, "If we break a piece of machinery and don't have a spare part, but someone else [some other distillery] does, they'll lend it to us until we get our replacement in." Now certainly at the level of marketing, the competition is fierce, but at the production level, the men who actually make America's classic whiskeys have a cordiality, respect, and often even a fondness for each other—as we now have for them.

We can only hope that they approve of the way in which we have told their story and that you, the readers, will enjoy reading this book as much as we have enjoyed writing it.

Acknowledgments

The content of this book has benefitted enormously from the warm and helpful co-operation of numerous people—indeed, more people than we could possibly mention here. We would particularly like to acknowledge the generous assistance of the following persons: F. Booker Noe (of Jim Beam), Jimmy Russell (of Wild Turkey), Bill Samuels (of Maker's Mark), Al Young (of Seagram's), Chris Morris and Mike Veach (of United Distillers), Jerry Dalton (of Barton Distilling), Michael Sonne and Craig Beam (of Heaven Hill), Gary Gayheart (of Leestown), Phil Lynch and Lois Mateus (of Brown-Forman), Roger Brashears, Mary Baird, and Gerald Hamilton (of Jack Daniel's), Dave Backus (of George Dickel), Flaget Nally, Dixie Hibbs, and Mary Hite (all of the Oscar Getz Museum of Whiskey History), Elizabeth Board and Matthew Vellucci (of the Distilled Spirits Council).

1

The Story of Whiskey in America

The Old Country

When Americans travel in foreign countries, we learn to appreciate anew many things that we normally take for granted in the busy rush of our everyday lives. Foreign travel can serve to make us take pride in those uniquely American products which visitors to our country immediately notice. Indoor plumbing which works is one thing. Peanut butter is another. Those who have become accustomed to a certain whiskey scan the bottles located behind the bars in restaurants and pubs, looking for a familiar label. People seek out the places which carry their favorite American whiskey, and they ask for it by names which are as famous and as distinctively American as the names of George Washington, Benjamin Franklin, Daniel Boone, and Davy Crockett—Wild Turkey, Jack Daniel's, Jim Beam, Evan Williams, I. W. Harper, Old Fitzgerald, or George Dickel. Very few countries of the world have the distinction of being identified closely with the spirits which they produce—Scotch from Scotland, of course, vodka from Russia, gin from England, and Canadian blended whiskey.

American whiskey—principally, Kentucky Bourbon and Tennessee Whiskey—is one of those products which is known and identi-

1

fied world-wide as a uniquely American product. Just as Scotch whisky can be made only in Scotland, Kentucky Bourbon and Tennessee Sipping Whiskey can be made only in the United States. Although the whiskeys which are made today are the result of sophisticated modern plants, the basic processes have remained unchanged for hundreds of years. The American whiskeys available today are, in many cases, essentially the same as those available to early settlers in America. This is the story of how such whiskey came to be made in America and how the famous names such as Jim Beam, Jack Daniels, Wild Turkey, and many others became a part of American culture.

Whiskey and the South

Nearly all of the whiskey made in the United States today is made in the southern states, and, more importantly, the origin of the whiskey which is recognized around the world today as distinctively American originated in the southern United States. So, in an important sense, the story of American whiskey is part of the story of the South. There are historical and geological reasons why American whiskey originated in the southern states—proximity to grain sources and abundant, soft limestone water are among them. Cultural factors were also important. As we will see, in the seventeenth and eighteenth centuries, the South attracted a large percentage of the Scottish, Irish, and English settlers to come to this country, with a major population of French along the Mississippi Delta. In the eighteenth and nineteenth centuries, when considerable numbers of Scandinavians, Germans, Slavs, and Italians immigrated to America, they located in the northern states. Thus, the white population of the South—from the sixteenth to the mid-twentieth century—was much more homogenous both racially and culturally than that of the North.

The South has produced a disproportionately large share of what is recognized today as distinctively American culture. The enormous influence of the South on American life has persisted from the very beginning of the country. Most of the major figures of the American revolution and early leaders, including four of the first five presi-

Courtesy of The Oscar Getz Museum

One of George Washington's stills

dents of the United States, were from the South. American whiskey is one of several important cultural contributions, recognized around the world as distinctively American, whose origin is traced to the southern United States. Although distilling came to America from the 'Old Country' and although the earliest centers of distilling included Pennsylvania and New York, whiskey making found its natural home in the southern states.

The Southern contribution to American culture is most dramatically illustrated perhaps in American literature—the roll call of major Southern authors is amazing. Although it is always dangerous to list names because of the possibility of omitting some major figure, the list which instantly springs to mind is impressive indeed: Truman Capote, Thomas Chivers, Kate Chopin, James Dickey, William Faulkner, Joel Chandler Harris, Sidney Lanier, Harper Lee, Carson McCullers, Margaret Mitchell, Flannery O'Connor, Walker Percy,

Edgar Allan Poe, Katherine Anne Porter, William Styron, Mark Twain, Thomas Wolfe, and, in a more contemporary vein, John Grisham, Larry McMurtry, and Tom Wolfe.

The South also served as the cradle for the birth of most of what is regarded as distinctively American music. While early Americans settled along the eastern seaboard in the mid-Atlantic and northeastern states still looked to the 'Old Country' for much of their culture, Southerners were busy producing new music which was uniquely American. The most accomplished performing artists—symphony orchestras and opera companies—were located in large Northern cities and performed European music. On the level of popular music, even vaudeville was an import from Europe. Meanwhile, with the mingling of black and white influences, the South produced the music which is distinctively American in origin, including rhythm and blues, jazz, country and western, rock 'n' roll, and, of course, bluegrass which is derived from Celtic music and which is another area of Scotch-Irish influence on American culture.

When we think of the most valued and prized products of human endeavor ever produced in this country, we would need to include such notables as Faulkner's *Light in August,* Twain's *Huckleberry Finn,* Mitchell's *Gone With the Wind,* Styron's *Sophie's Choice,* Hank Williams's 'Your Cheatin' Heart,' and Chuck Berry's 'Johnny B. Goode.'

The South was also the origin of the only musical instrument generally recognized to have originated in the United States—the five-string banjo. Although the banjo itself can be traced to African origins, Joel Walker, a Virginian, is credited with adding the fifth string, the 'drone' string, which gives the five-string its distinctive sound and unique identity. Country music, the banjo, rhythm and blues, peanut butter, Kentucky Bourbon and Tennessee whiskey are all distinctively American products which find their origins in the South. When the roll of honor is called of those most excellent products ever manufactured in this country (or perhaps any country), Kentucky Bourbon and Tennessee Sippin' Whiskey would have to be included somewhere near the top of the list.

Whiskey and Daily Life

Whiskey found its way into the daily lives of the western European settlers in America from the very beginning of their exploration of America. The early settlers who came to America brought whatever they could from their European homelands—as much clothing and kitchenware and as many personal items as possible. They also brought with them whatever knowledge and habits had characterized their lives in the Old Country. The architecture, recipes, tools, and methods of agriculture and social customs of the early colonists copied those from European countries. In some cases, the old ways of doing things worked well for dealing with the new situations and problems confronted by the settlers in the new country. In other cases, new ways had to be improvised.

The development of a unique way of making American whiskey is a good illustration of how the original knowledge from the Old Country was modified and adapted by the ingenuity of early Americans to produce something which is now completely American.

Water of Life

The practice of fermentation of fruits to make wine is, of course, older than the business of producing distilled spirits and was known to most ancient peoples. While history does not record the beginnings of the distillation of spirits, we do have evidence that the ancient Chinese and Greeks had some knowledge of the process of distillation. During the 'Dark Ages,' Arab scholars preserved much of the accumulated knowledge of ancient civilizations, then later passed it on to western European countries—including knowledge of the distillation of spirits. On a more practical level, the ancient Celts in Northern Europe and somewhat later, in the British Isles, were responsible for producing a distilled spirit from handmade, copper 'pot stills,' a drink they called, in Gaelic, *uisge beatha* or *uisgebaugh,* meaning 'water of life.' The result of this process, which has remained essentially unaltered for centuries, is what is now known as Scotch whisky. (For an account of the history of Scotch and of the present-day distillers of single-malt whisky, see *Single-Malt Whiskies of Scotland*.)

The careful reader will have noticed that when we have talked about American whiskey, we have spelled 'whiskey' w-h-i-s-k-E-y, and when we have talked about Scotch whisky, we have spelled 'whisky' w-h-i-s-k-y (with no e). Scots and Canadians spell 'whisky' with no 'e' while Irish and Americans use an 'e.' So it is Scotch or Canadian 'whisky' and 'whiskies' but Irish or Bourbon 'whiskey' and 'whiskeys'. Yet a few American distilleries have a tradition, which they scrupulously maintain, of always spelling 'whisky' without an 'e' (see chapters 3 and 4).

The appellation 'water of life' is apt since whisky was, and in many places remains, an essential component of the everyday, common life of the people of Scotland. Whiskey (and beer and wine) was also very much a part of the daily lives of the early European settlers in America who brought the knowledge of how to distill whisky as well as their small pot stills with them. Although the Indians of the southwestern United States and Mexico probably knew about distilling from the Aztecs (who distilled mescal from the fermented sap of magney), there is no evidence that Indians in the eastern United States knew about distilling at all.

The story of Scotch whisky is particularly important for American whiskey since it was the Scotch-Irish—descendants of the Scots who had settled in what is now Northern Ireland—who were primarily responsible for the beginnings of the process of making distilled spirits in America. Although there were also important early Dutch and German distillers (the earliest documented operating still was in Dutch New York), the most significant contribution came from the Scotch-Irish. The trail of whiskey distillation in America is a trail which follows the location and then the relocation of these Scotch-Irish as they moved inland with their pot stills from the East coast.

The Scotch-Irish

The first record of distilled spirits in what would later become the United States was on Staten Island, in Dutch New Amsterdam, in 1640—just 33 years after the English first landed at Jamestown, Virginia. For the next hundred years or so, rum was the most popular commercial distilled spirit in the colonies. Rum was distilled in

J. T. S. Brown Distillery, Anderson County, Kentucky, 1900

Courtesy of The Oscar Getz Museum

dozens of New England distilleries from molasses shipped from the sugar cane plantations in the West Indies. Meanwhile, the Scotch-Irish, fleeing famines in 1717–18 and again in 1727–28 continued their migration to America through ports in New York and Philadelphia. Because of their Scottish Presbyterian religion, those Scotch-Irish who attempted to settle in New England received a hostile reception from the Puritans, and eventually because of the religious tolerance of the Quakers in western Pennsylvania, most Scotch-Irish found their way there, and thence to western Virginia and western North Carolina to the south.

My Kingdom for a Horse

Distilling whiskey was a routine event in the everyday lives of the Scotch-Irish settlers. By the early eighteenth century, there were literally thousands of small individually-owned pot stills with which the settlers made whiskey for their own consumption and for barter with their neighbors. Shakespeare's account of Richard III's offer to barter his kingdom for a horse is perhaps the most well-known offer to barter in recorded history, but probably more deals have been struck involving the trade of whiskey than any other single item—even horses. During the early eighteenth century, there are records of whiskey being used as pledges to build churches, as barter for mules and horses, crops, real estate, and even slaves. Whiskey was also commonly used instead of wages. The General Ledgers of the old Walter (Wattie, a cousin of Daniel Boone) Boone distillery in what was then Nelson County, Kentucky, now in the possession of Nancy Samuels and Bill Samuels Jr., President of Maker's Mark, indicate that Thomas Lincoln, father of Abraham, frequently drew whiskey against his wages for working at the distillery in the 1790s. Carl Sandburg, noted biographer of Lincoln, reports that when Thomas Lincoln sold his Kentucky farm and left for Indiana and then Illinois in 1816, he received 400 gallons (ten barrels) of whiskey and $20 in payment. Now Sandburg alleges that Thomas was "not much of a drinking man," a description which is not consistent with the oral tradition in central Kentucky. Perhaps Thomas Lincoln just realized what a valuable commodity the Kentucky whiskey would be as he moved north where it would be relatively scarce. How much of the whiskey was used for personal consumption and how much as barter to help locate the Lincoln family in its new home is not recorded.

Another practice in early Kentucky which involved the use of whiskey was what has become known as 'treating.' Long before the rise of television and the 'sound bite' for political campaigns, politicians running for election realized the importance of making a direct and effective appeal to the voters. When Kentucky was still a part of Virginia, frontier politicians often appealed to prospective voters by offering them free whiskey. Such 'treating' often even occurred on election day. Virginia tried to stop the practice, but there is evidence that it continued even after Kentucky became a state.

The whiskey was distilled from some corn but primarily from rye, an old world grain which will grow in poor soil and was brought to America from northern Europe. Rye seemed well-suited to the soil of Pennsylvania. It quickly became the principal grain of the area, and rye whiskey became a very popular drink.

Although there were thousands of individual pot stills in which people were making whiskey in the western counties of the colonies, the actual volume was small, and the western counties of Pennsylvania and Virginia were far removed from the lucrative Eastern markets where, from 1700 to 1750, rum dominated the market. However, western settlers quickly discovered that it was far easier to transport barrels of whiskey to the Eastern markets than to ship tons of grain, and the market for whiskey was a stable, steadily rising one with relatively quick and easy profits. By the early 1780s, settlers in Kentucky and Tennessee were taking whiskey down the Ohio and Tennessee Rivers to the Mississippi and then down to New Orleans—a trip which lasted as long as three months. Records for 1810 indicate that Kentucky, Tennessee, Virginia, North Carolina, Ohio, and Pennsylvania produced *millions* of gallons of whiskey. By 1825, there are reports of *hundreds* of flatboats of various sizes—from small one-man skiffs to large barges—in New Orleans with lumber, cotton, pork, tobacco, corn, potatoes, and whiskey from Kentucky and Tennessee. A bushel of corn was worth only about 50 cents while the three to five gallons of whiskey which could be made from that bushel of corn were worth as much as $2 per gallon. Whiskey was the commodity which offered the greatest value by volume or weight for transportation.

Now That's a Good Whiskey

At the same time, consumers were also becoming well-informed 'smart shoppers'—they became concerned with proof and quality of whiskey. Early methods for determining proof were fairly primitive. The designation of 'proof,' which indicates the percentage of alcoholic content, came from the method of testing whiskey by mixing it with gunpowder in a shallow pan and then lighting it. If the whiskey had too little alcohol (and thus too much water) the mixture would not burn and the gunpowder would not flash; it was of poor 'gunpowder proof.' However, it there was enough alcohol in the whiskey, the whiskey would burn and then light the gunpowder which would flash, an indication of proper proof.

Proof could also be determined to the practiced eye by the quick and easy method of shaking whiskey in a clear glass and examining the 'blebs' which formed on the surface. With a whiskey of high proof, the blebs (small bubbles forming what is now called a 'bead') remain on the surface. A good strong, lasting bead which covers most or all of the surface of the whiskey in the glass prompts the satisfied exclamation, 'Now that's a good whiskey!' With a whiskey of low proof, the surface is flat with no bead or with one which is non-distinct or short-lasting.

A beneficial consequence of the otherwise much-hated Excise tax of 1791 was the imposition of standards for measuring proof of whiskey. The hydrometer was adopted by the government as the official instrument to be used for determining proof, and each 'excise man' brought one along when he came to determine the proof of the whiskey for tax purposes. The hydrometer was soon accepted by the entire industry for determining proof.

American-made whiskey from American-grown grain was beginning to make its way into the American marketplace, American history, American culture, and American hearts.

Bourbon Whiskey

It's surprising how few people know what Bourbon is or what distinguishes it from other distilled spirits. We will describe the process of making Bourbon in detail in the next chapter; however, in order to tell the story of how Bourbon first came to be made, it is important to understand exactly what Bourbon is. Currently, Bourbon is defined as whiskey which is distilled at no more than 160 proof from a fermented mash which must be at least 51 percent corn and aged in new, charred oak barrels for at least two years. The story of how and where the first Bourbon was made and by whom is one rich in folklore and filled with colorful characters. There is also a fair amount of controversy and friendly competition over the telling of the story since different locations and descendants of different families have laid claim to the origin of Bourbon. The requirements concerning proof and aging are relatively recent—the result of the federal Bottled in Bond Act of 1897. So, when we enquire about the origin of the very first Bourbon, we are really looking for the first whiskey distilled primarily from a fermented corn mash and aged in charred barrels.

There seems to be little doubt that the whiskey produced in western Pennsylvania, the subject of the first Federal Excise Tax on Whiskey, the Whiskey Rebellion, and Washington's Watermelon Army, was not Bourbon. Although some whiskey might have been produced from corn in western Pennsylvania at that time, the principal grain was rye. However, large numbers of Scotch-Irish had continued, from the Monongahela River Valley in Pennsylvania on down the Ohio River, and had found themselves in corn country in northern and central Kentucky (from an American Indian word meaning 'dark and bloody land' because of the bloody wars between different tribes in the area). These settlers in Kentucky brought their pot stills with them. Along with an abundant supply of fairly soft, iron-free limestone water, they then had all of the ingredients needed to make Bourbon whiskey.

The First Bourbon

The earliest records of distilling in Kentucky date from the last few decades of the eighteenth century with various competing claims for the oldest still in Kentucky. The Pepper Distillery, founded by Elijah Pepper and located just outside Lexington, Kentucky, off Frankfort Pike, is alleged to have started distillation in 1776. The distillery produced a product labelled 'Old 1776' and used, as part of its advertising campaign, the claim that it was 'Born with the Republic.' Other claims have been made on behalf of John Ritchie, who is supposed to have built a still just outside Bardstown, Kentucky, in 1777, and Henry Hudson Wathen, who is supposed to have built a still near Lebanon, Kentucky, in 1788. Other historians of early Kentucky bestow the honor of having made the first whiskey in Kentucky upon Evan Williams who is reported to have made whiskey as early as 1783 from his still in Louisville. In what was then Lincoln County, Jacob Myers is known to have operated a still prior to 1781. The written documentation for this claim is ironic since, in 1781, Myers ran for election to the Virginia House of Burgesses against Benjamin Logan, an 'Indian fighter' of some renown, and attempted to use his whiskey to buy votes. Myers lost the election.

For most of these stories there is little documentation, only oral tradition, to support a definitive claim that any one of these men was the first distiller in Kentucky; so the controversy is likely to continue. We may never be able to conclusively identify 'the first distiller' any more than we will be able to identify 'the first farmer.' What few historians there were at the time did not regard information about making whiskey as something which deserved special attention. It was simply a part of everyday life. In any case, none of the whiskey produced by any of these figures would have really been considered *Bourbon* whiskey in the modern sense, since although it's likely that the whiskey producers used a fermented mash mixture of corn, rye, and barley, there is no mention of any of this whiskey being aged in charred barrels.

The Use of Charred Barrels

The use of charred oak barrels for aging whiskey is one of the most distinctive and controversial features of Bourbon. Exactly how this aging process came about is a story which belongs more to legend than to history, so we can only speculate, as others have done, as to how this process was begun. Nevertheless, some speculations are more reasonable than others, and the circumstances and conditions of the times allow us to make a some pretty good guesses about the origin of aging whiskey in charred barrels. Some writers have attributed the discovery of this process to chance—the accidental result of some clumsy cooper burning barrel staves while heating them and then later noticing the enhanced quality of the whiskey. We think that it's more plausible that the use of charred barrels was a deliberate choice, the result of existing knowledge plus some simple trial and error.

Those writers who have attributed the use of charred barrels to luck or accident have not considered carefully what must have been part of the common knowledge of the early settlers. In the abstract, the business of aging whiskey in charred oak barrels might seem to be so bizarre that we might wonder, 'How did anyone ever possibly think of *that*?' But in the context of the early settlers' knowledge, aging in charred barrels is not so bizarre after all.

In the first place, aging itself was a natural consequence of the conditions of the time. Distillation was for the most part seasonal, depending primarily upon the weather and the harvesting of grains. Given the scarcity of goods which existed on the frontier along with the severity of the winters, it was necessary to store goods for the winter—including whiskey. Only slow modes of transportation were available—by river boat or by wagons drawn by teams of horses or mules. Such wagons carrying whiskey as well as other 'dry' goods were driven by *teamsters,* the origin of a name which still resonates today in organized labor. It sometimes took several months for goods to reach their destination. Since the most dramatic effects of aging whiskey take place in the first year, it's reasonable to suppose that almost anyone could tell the difference in quality between whiskey right out of the still and that shipped to distance places, and the news would have spread very quickly. So, the process of aging itself and the obvious benefits for the whiskey were probably common knowledge for some time. It is also very reasonable to suppose that knowledge of the benefits of aging upon whiskey was something which the Scotch-Irish brought with them to the new world. In any case, it is unlikely that much aging at all took place before 1800 since what few references there are to whiskey in written records describe the whiskey as 'made this year' or, in some cases, 'made last year.'

The aromatic effects of burning wood were known and understood as well as the process of obtaining various gums and syrups from trees. Chewing upon the sweet twigs of some trees was the fore-runner of the practice of brushing teeth. The practice of adding 'sweeteners' to distilled spirits was an old, established one. Finally, the effects of using charcoal as a filter to 'purify' liquids has been known since ancient times, and barrels used to transport liquids were charred in the belief that this would keep the liquids from 'going bad'—becoming putrid. It seems reasonable to suppose that once whiskey started to become a viable commercial product, producers and distributors began to experiment with various ways of softening and making more palatable the raw, fiery taste of the alcohol and protecting that taste. Using fire to gain access to and release the beneficial effects of the resins and sugars in the wood emerges as a reasonable process to try, given other knowledge which must have been commonplace on the frontier.

In addition to allowing the sugars in the wood to mellow the whiskey, charring the barrels is also a method of protecting the quality of the whiskey during aging. One cause for barrels of whiskey 'going bad' was discovered to be small bubbles or 'blisters' on the inside of the barrel where the sap from the freshly sawn wood would concentrate. If the whiskey were absorbed into the blisters the concentration could actually putrefy the whiskey instead of mellowing it. One of the earliest known accounts documenting the use of charring for barrels by Harrison Hall in 1818 describes the use of charred barrels as a method of smoothing the inside of the barrels and protecting against the blisters of sap which threatened the quality of the whiskey. It was a very early, and obviously effective, means of quality control.

Early historians credited the Reverend Elijah Craig with making the first Bourbon near Georgetown, Kentucky. Craig was a well-known and highly regarded Baptist minister who was also one of the frontier's first enterprising capitalists. He was a major landowner and ran a grist mill and a paper mill as well as a still. Craig has now become a legendary figure who is credited by many people with being responsible for first using the modern grain formula for Bourbon—a mixture of corn, rye, and barley—as well as being the first to use charred barrels for aging the whiskey. Craig is a convenient figure to identify from the murky past with such notable achievements because there are written tax records which do prove that Craig was actually producing whiskey in the early 1790s, and because Craig is such a colorful character since he was a 'Hellfire and brimstone' Baptist preacher. Some current historians speculate that the story of Craig's contribution to early whiskey making was embellished by the distillers of the late 1800s to provide themselves with something of a moral 'cover story' and to protect themselves from the Prohibitionists. Although it makes for a good story, we find nothing to confirm that Craig was the first person to make Bourbon or use charred barrels. However, he is just as likely as dozens of other possible candidates for the honor. What is interesting about the story of Elijah Craig is what it tells us about the rela-

Courtesy of United Distillers

The Cascade Distillery Warehouse, ca. 1890

tionship between religion and whiskey on the early frontier and in early American culture in general. There is no record of the slightest hint of disapproval about Craig or other religious figures being involved in the whiskey business or indeed, actually drinking the whiskey. Opposition to whiskey by religious groups and other temperance groups was to come much later, in the nineteenth century.

The first public record we have been able to find of the use of the name 'Bourbon' to describe whiskey comes from a newspaper advertisement for 'Bourbon Whiskey' in 1821 in the *Western Citizen,* the newspaper in Paris, Kentucky, in Bourbon County. The most commonly used original designation, in the 1820s and 1830s, was 'Old Bourbon Whiskey.' By the 1840s, the designation had become simply 'Bourbon Whiskey,' but, of course, from then to the present day, every distiller will insist that he made it in 'the old' way.

How Bourbon Got Its Name

Today we are used to a county being a relatively small area, headed by a town known as the 'county seat,' with a court house and the offices of county government. There is indeed such a Bourbon County in Kentucky today, but this is not the Bourbon County from which the whiskey got its name. At the time of the revolutionary war, all of what is now the state of Kentucky was simply *part* of what was known as Fincastle County which was, in turn, part of Virginia. Colonial territories and counties could be very large in those days. During the War for Independence, the French and King Louis XVI were, of course, the main source of foreign support for the colonists in their fight against George III of England, and King Louis XVI was a member of the Bourbon family. Following the war, the victorious colonists (particularly those in Virginia where the final battle of Yorktown had been fought, when the French forces were decisive in Washington's victory over Cornwallis) honored the French by naming numerous towns and counties (and, one can safely assume, babies as well) after the French. Bourbon County, which at the time comprised *all* of the area which is now northern and central Kentucky, was named after the French king by the State Assembly of Virginia in 1785. Evidence of just how uniquely *American* Bourbon Whiskey is and also evidence of just how provincial (in a very ironic sense) the British are is that the only entry for the word 'Bourbon' in the *Oxford English Dictionary, the* most authoritative reference dictionary of the English language, contains no meaning connected to the whiskey at all. The only meaning provided in the *OED* refers to the royal family of France.

At the same time as the names of Bourbon County and Kentucky were first becoming well-known designations for these areas of the country, the whiskey produced there was also becoming well known. 'Kentucky Bourbon' became a standard generic way of identifying this whiskey, distinguishing it from Pennsylvania Rye, Maryland Rye, or New England Rum. As the original Bourbon County was divided, time and again, into smaller units, the name for the distinctive kind of whiskey stuck, and thus, today, we have Kentucky Bourbon. In fact, Bourbon could then legally be made in other places than Kentucky, as it can today, but it is not '*Kentucky* Bourbon.' Ironically, the modern-day Bourbon County, Kentucky, just a very small part of the original Bourbon County which gave Bourbon Whiskey its name, is dry (as are many other counties in Kentucky), and no whiskey has been made there for quite some time, at least not legally.

Tennessee

In some ways the early exploration and settlement of Tennessee by white settlers paralleled that of Kentucky; in other ways it was quite different. De Soto had explored the Tennessee River Valley in his famous quest for the Fountain of Youth as early as 1540, but permanent settlers were very few until the middle of the eighteenth century.

Originally, Tennessee was part of the Colony of North Carolina which stretched all the way to the Mississippi River. Settlers moved from Virginia and North Carolina west into Tennessee, but the movement west was much slower in Tennessee than in Kentucky. The relatively easy river traffic along the Ohio and Monongahela Rivers encouraged the move into Kentucky; the rough and inaccessible Appalachian Mountains made the move into Tennessee much more difficult. One of the few routes through the mountains, in the northeast corner of present day Tennessee is the Cumberland Gap, through which Daniel Boone, working for the Transylvania Company, blazed the famous Wilderness Trail in the late 1770s.

While the colonists along the eastern seaboard were primarily concerned about taxes and their relationship with England, the early settlers in western North Carolina, in what was to become Tennessee, were mainly concerned with their survival. They wanted protection from hostile Indians—the Cherokee and the Chickasaw, the Mound Builders. Limited resources and limited access to the region meant that the Colony of North Carolina provided little or no help to the early settlers of Tennessee (as we have seen was also the case in western Virginia in what was to become Kentucky). As a result, the early Tennesseans, in the familiar frontier spirit of independence and defiance, began a series of moves which led to forming their own government.

In what is one of the earliest written constitutions among American settlers, the pioneers along the Watauga River in Tennessee formed the Watauga Association in 1772, a free and independent state, which had its own legislature and sheriff. In 1780 pioneers who had come down the Cumberland River to Fort Nashborough (Nashville) signed the Cumberland Compact which established a legislature with elected representatives and a court system.

In 1784, three counties in what is now eastern Tennessee, "succeeded" (sic.) from North Carolina and formed the free and independent State of Franklin. John Sevier, a Revolutionary War hero, was named Governor of the State of Franklin. A political crisis was developing for the young, struggling United States government. Neither North Carolina nor the federal government of the United States was prepared to deal directly with this direct challenge. In a series of astute political moves, North Carolina 'gave' the entire Tennessee region of North Carolina (including the State of Franklin) to the United States in 1789. This area was named a federal territory, and then became the 16th state in 1796. John Sevier was the first Governor.

Many of these early settlers in Tennessee were from the same stock and brought with them the same knowledge, customs and traditions as the settlers in Kentucky. This included the knowledge of how to make whiskey, and the early process of whiskey-making in Tennessee did not differ from what we have described in early Kentucky. However, some time in the early nineteenth century, distillers in Lincoln County, Tennessee, began to filter their whiskey through *several feet* of fresh maple charcoal as a part of the process—*before* putting the whiskey into barrels. This method, which was to become distinctive of Tennessee Whiskey, was known as the Lincoln County Process. The earliest documented use of the Lincoln County Process occurred in a distillery owned and operated by Alfred Eaton in Tullahoma, Tennessee, in 1825. (We discuss this process more completely in our chapter on Tennessee whiskeys, Chapter 4 below.)

The Tennessee River provides the largest major waterway through Tennessee. Unlike the Ohio River, which follows a slow, smooth arc around the present-day northern boundary of Kentucky into the Mississippi River, the Tennessee cuts a meandering path which begins in southeastern Tennessee and flows first southwest, into what is now Alabama, then west, across the northern part of that state, then northwest, across Tennessee, from south to north, and then into Kentucky where it empties into the Ohio River at Paducah. It was no simple accident that the Tennessee River Valley, which reaches into seven southern states, was chosen by Congress for the site of the first federal project for flood control and the generation of electricity. The Tennessee Valley Authority, created by Congress in 1933 and covering an area almost as large as England, now contains more than 40 different dams to control and manage one of the most powerful sources of natural power in the country.

Whiskey and Social Life

The early colonists brought the knowledge of making beer, wine, and spirits, as well as the patterns of behavior surrounding the consumption of these beverages, with them from Europe. Even the Pilgrims brought whiskey with them on the Mayflower. We have already indicated that the knowledge of distilling whiskey and the pot stills necessary for making whiskey were brought to America by the early colonists, but the attitudes and social institutions involving the making, distribution, and consumption of whiskey in the colonies mirror those of Europe as well. The early settlers believed, as their European ancestors had, that whiskey had great medicinal powers, and physicians prescribed whiskey in various concoctions for an assortment of different ailments. Distilled spirits were initially made from various fermented fruits. Applejack, distilled from fermented, 'hard' apple cider, was a favorite. Although the consumption rate was very high by our standards, the colonists controlled the commercial and even the private, personal consumption of alcohol very ardently and very strictly.

The taverns and inns which served beer, wine, and spirits to the early colonists were at the center of social life in the colonial period of American history, and it is impossible to separate the story of early American history, the story of American whiskey, and the story of these taverns and inns. The earliest taverns were located alongside the roads and paths as convenient places for travelers to rest, and the different local political authorities had the responsibilities for regulating these taverns and inns. And regulate them they did. A study of the regulations controlling taverns and spirits offers some subtle insights into early life in the American colonies. For example, two different kinds of licenses were issued for places selling beer and spirits—the ordinary license allowed only the sale of drink and food and expressly prohibited any entertainment (especially gambling) and the other, of course, allowed gambling. The 'ordinary' licenses created places which became known as 'Ordinaries' which were to become the centers of social life in the early colonies.

Ordinaries were very respectable places where the most wealthy and respectable colonists dined and passed the time in conversation, while taverns were quite rowdy by colonial standards, with singing and gambling. Both Ordinaries and taverns were regulated quite rigorously by local governments—including their locations, prices, and hours of operation. Overindulgence was strictly discouraged and regulations controlled not only how much whiskey a person could be served but even how long a person could sit in the Ordinary or tavern to drink without also being served food.

Whiskey and Religion

Some of the restrictions placed on the operation of Ordinaries are quite interesting and very informative about colonial life. For example, in many locations Ordinaries had to be located within a certain distance of a church and were required to have hours of operation on Sunday. No, these requirements were not to allow the clergy and the churchgoers to keep an eye on the customers. The clergy and the churchgoers were the main clientele of the Ordinaries. When the only means of travel were either horseback or carriage, and when the parishioners (and many times the clergy) had to travel many miles to the church (and frequently through cold and inclement weather), the churchgoers needed a place to rest and refresh themselves (and perhaps to civilly discuss the sermon or conduct a little business) before returning home. Members of the vestry (the governing board of the Anglican and later, the Episcopa-

Courtesy of United Distillers

The George Dickel Cascade Distillery, ca. 1900

lian church) might hold meetings at the Ordinary (remember the churches were probably not heated). Weddings and funerals were also occasions when having the Ordinary located near the church was a matter of great convenience. So, religion and whiskey were very closely associated in the early colonies in the seventeenth and eighteenth centuries.

Whiskey and Politics

The Ordinaries also served as the center of political activity in the early colonies. In most places, Ordinaries were built long before courthouses were; so trials were frequently conducted in many Ordinaries. The serving of food and whiskey would be interrupted while court was in session, and would resume when court was concluded. Political discussions and various meetings of civic groups took place in Ordinaries, taverns, and inns throughout the colonies, and Ordinaries frequently served as polling places for elections. Various local committees and groups would meet at the Ordinary, including the local militia.

Ordinaries became so important to the life of the colonists in the mid-eighteenth century that some colonies even *required* counties and towns to have an Ordinary, and the counties or towns had to pay fines if they did not maintain a proper Ordinary. This arrangement was the beginning in America of the now long standing practice of negotiated business between private enterprise and local governments. The enterprising businessmen who owned and operated the Ordinaries would attempt to negotiate 'deals' with the local town or county governments which involved such perks as free land for the location of the Ordinary, free land for a farm, or special tax rates.

In the first half of the seventeenth century, beer, wine, cider, and brandy were the most popular drinks. In the last part of the seventeenth century, as a result of the infamous triangular trade of rum and slaves, rum and drinks containing rum—known as Grog, Toddy, Flip, and Sling—became popular. Making these drinks was the source of an American expression which seems to have become permanently etched in American English. Metal pokers, called 'loggerheads,' with a rounded end would be heated in the open fire and then used to heat the mixed drinks so customers could personalize their drinks according to their individual preferences. Customers might sometimes brandish these red-hot pokers at one another during heated political arguments. Hence, the expression 'being at loggerheads' came to mean being at extreme odds or having irreconcilable differences with another person. American-made whiskey began to replace rum as the most popular distilled spirit in the Colonies in the second half of the eighteenth century.

Many famous individuals and events involved with the American Revolution were associated, in one way or another, with whiskey, ordinaries, taverns, and inns. Every famous figure associated with the American Revolution was surely a frequent customer at such establishments. George Washington operated his own distillery at his home, Mount Vernon, for a number of years where he made rye whiskey as well as peach and apple brandy. What is thought to be Washington's still was captured by 'revenue agents' in 1939 during a raid on an illegal distilling operation at the home of a black family who were direct descendants of slaves of George Washington. The handsome, hand-made copper still was marked "made in Bristol, England, 1783." The still was on display for some time both at the Smithsonian and in the offices of the Internal Revenue Service in Washington, D.C.

Taverns and inns also served as the locations for many famous meetings and events. Students from the College of William and Mary organized Phi Beta Kappa, the oldest and still most prestigious honor society, at Raleigh's Tavern, in Williamsburg, Virginia, in 1776. Plans were made for the famous Boston Tea Party in a Boston tavern, and Paul Revere and his friends, Samuel Adams and John Hancock, also concocted the plan to warn Boston of the coming of the British in a Boston tavern. The first battle of the Revolutionary War started at Buckman's Tavern in Lexington, Massachusetts, when the Minutemen were fired upon by the British troops which had been sent to disperse them. Many famous figures either owned taverns or worked in them, including such notables as Patrick Henry, Samuel Adams, Ethan Allen, and much later, of course, Abraham Lincoln. The delegates from the thirteen colonies to the First Continental Congress met in the City Tavern in Philadelphia as Thomas Jefferson worked on the Declaration of Independence in another tavern. Ordinaries, taverns, and inns were centers of social and political life in the colonies, and it was from the activities surrounding these drinking establishments that the United States was begun.

Whiskey and American History

The story of American whiskey is as intriguing and instructive as any part of American history. We are also beginning to see how the history of American whiskey can teach us much about the history of America. The story of American whiskey is interwoven with the very birth, development, and growth of the United States as a country. It is a story of American agriculture, American business and commerce, American transportation, American politics and prominent American politicians, American geography and geology, American law and law enforcement, American social customs and institutions, and, sadly, even American political corruption.

Whiskey has figured prominently in several major political crises in the history of America. Whiskey served as a catalyst for the first serious challenge to the unity and stability of the federal government. The conflict was between the power of the then new federal government and the autonomy of the individual states. The crisis occurred when the federalist, Alexander Hamilton, Secretary of the Treasury under President George Washington, convinced Congress to impose a federal excise tax on whiskey and George Washington formed an army to enforce the tax. American whiskey may be unique in having prompted *two* amendments to the Constitution of the United States—the eighteenth, creating Prohibition, and the twenty-first, abolishing Prohibition. The period of Prohibition was arguably one of the most difficult periods in the life of this country. As we will also see later, the rise of the America whiskey industry even had some influence on ending the slave trade, when Bourbon began to supplant rum as the drink of choice in the American Colonies.

The story of American whiskey is also a story of the American frontier. The growth and development of the production, transportation, distribution, and marketing of American whiskey had as much influence upon the settlement of the western frontier as did the railroads, cattle raising, or firearms. However, though most schoolchildren learn about the importance of railroads and cattle in grade school, the influence of conservative political and religious groups (the lingering influence of Carry Nation and the Women's Christian Temperance Union) has suppressed teaching about the importance of whiskey to early American history and particularly to settling the frontier. Aside from the occasional casual mention of saloons in books and movies, little serious attention is given to whiskey as a commercial product or to the various economic, political and social institutions interconnected with whiskey. But think for a moment. When a cowboy walked into a saloon in Texas or Kansas or Wyoming and ordered a bottle or shot of 'red eye' whiskey, what was he ordering? Where did it come from? And how did it get there? When we explore questions like these in the history of American whiskey, we find that the connections of whiskey with the settlement of the West are as intricate and surprising as the clues in a good mystery story. For example, 'red-eye' whiskey was the result of the development of a unique whiskey, originally Kentucky whiskey, later Kentucky Bourbon and Tennessee Sippin' whiskey, made through a unique process, principally from American corn and aged in charred oak barrels (which gives the whiskey its distinctive reddish color). The development of what was to become a rather standard process was the result of Old World knowledge and American ingenuity and innovation, a lot of trial and error, and luck.

The story of American whiskey is an important one which needs to be told to understand early American history, but it is also simply an interesting story in its own right. It's a story filled with important figures, colorful characters, and fascinating people. Even today, though the whiskey industry has become, for the most part, just that—an industry—the *people* now involved in the industry are among the most friendly, colorful, and delightful people we have ever met. However, in one respect, this ought not to be very surprising since the story of American whiskey is really a story of the American people. It was the people who made American whiskey what it is, and the making of the whiskey contributed, in part, to making us the people that we are.

Rum and Slaves

As we have indicated earlier, rum was by far the most popular distilled spirit of the earlier colonists since it was much more easily obtainable and much cheaper than spirits imported from Europe. From the mid-1600s until shortly after 1800, rum and the rum trade played a major role in shaping not only the drinking habits of the colonists and early Americans but also their economic, political and social practices. At first, rum was imported from the West Indies where it was originally made (rum is produced by distilling fermented molasses or sugarcane extract). By the early eighteenth century, the enterprising colonists had discovered that it was easier and more profitable to import the raw molasses and to distill the rum in this country. The New England rum trade was begun. By the mid-1700s there were dozens of rum distilleries clustered around Boston and Medford, Massachusetts, and Newport, Rhode Island. These New England rum distilleries supplied rum to all of the other colonies, and rum became a major item of barter not only in the colonies but abroad as well. Rum was so popular that it was supplied as a regular daily ration to members of the American Army and Navy, a practice which was continued until 1830 for the Army and 1862 for the Navy.

So, an entire industry was built around rum, and a major and essential part of that industry involved the infamous slave trade. Rum was one of the three vital commodities of the 'triangular trade': rum was shipped from New England to the gold coast of Africa (or to England and then to Africa) where it was traded for slaves. The rum ships then became slave runners, loaded with black prisoners who were transported to the West Indies or the southern colonies (in what has become known in the history books as 'the middle voyage' or 'the middle passage') where they were traded to the large sugar plantation owners for molasses which was then taken to New England to be made into rum to supply the colonists and to be shipped to Africa for more slaves. This was a lucrative arrangement: the ships never sailed empty. Although the sordid business of slavery is usually identified in history with the southern United States, many a fortune of New England families as well as the subsistence of hundreds or thousands of families of common New England laborers and sailors were owed to the slave trade. Euphemisms and misinformation abound here. Since the slaves were never brought to the New England colonies (and actually, rarely to the southern colonies directly), it was possible to describe the business as simply the rum trade. Even today, in various reference and history books concerning the business of trading rum for slaves, the reader will find the description under the heading of 'The Rum Trade' rather than 'The Slave Trade,' and the hands of the New Englanders are washed clean.

The Molasses Act

Because it was so lucrative, the rum/slave trade of New England, Africa and the West Indies became the flashpoint of the developing political struggle between the colonies and England. The French, Dutch, and Spanish colonies in the West Indies competed with the English colonies there on the one hand for the slaves which were being brought from Africa and on the other hand for the raw molasses which was being shipped to the English colonists in New England. The competitors were 'undercutting' the English on both ends of the deal, to the considerable profit of the New England traders. In 1733, the British Parliament finally passed the Molasses Act, an act of legislation specifically designed to force the American colonists to do business with the British colonies in the West Indies by imposing a prohibitive tax on any molasses imported into the American colonies except from the British colonies.

The Molasses Act was a way of ensuring that the British got what they thought was their fair share of the rum/slave trade. The Molasses Act was one of the first in a series of parliamentary Acts (including the Sugar and Stamp Acts) which imposed heavy taxation upon the colonies, and the pattern of defiance and non-compliance on the part of the colonists was set early with the Molasses Act. Those in the rum/slave trade ignored the British authorities, and continued to trade with the non-British colonies of the West Indies, and in one of those ironies which sometimes pop up in the study of history, shippers had to smuggle molasses while the shipment of slaves was quite legal. The rum/slave trade thus continued to flourish until long after the American Revolution. History books usually attribute the end of the sordid business of trading rum for slaves to the Embargo Act passed by the United Congress in 1807 (which prohibited the importation of foreign goods, including, of course, molasses) and to the abolition of the slave trade the following year by Congress. Usually unmentioned is the extent to which American-made whiskey from American-grown grains was beginning to supplant rum as the spirit of choice for Americans. The whiskeys made from American-grown rye and corn gradually became cheaper, more abundant and more readily available than rum, and another page in the history books was turned.

The Whiskey Rebellion

During the late 1770s and through the 1780s, the infant republic of the United States was in trouble, and the preservation of the union was, in the minds of many, in grave doubt. Considering the threat to the union which was later to come from the southern states and culminate in the formation of the Confederacy and the War Between the States, it might be reasonable to suppose that this early threat to the union of the Republic also came from the South. However, an even greater tension developed between the eastern states and the western states and territories. Since the eastern states were more settled, they shared more interests and had more common concerns, and the differences were much greater between the settled, 'civilized' eastern states and the 'wild' frontier lands. Geography also played an important role here. When we remember the primitive modes of transportation available at the time—horseback, carriage, and river boat—we can see how the states clustered along the eastern seaboard benefitted from the ease of transportation and communication and how the lands farther inland were relatively isolated because of the barriers posed by the Allegheny and Appalachian Mountains. At a time when life along the eastern seaboard was becoming fairly settled and when the social, political, and cultural affairs were being conducted in a safe and routine manner like that in the cities of western Europe, life on the frontier was bitter and hard, with constant threats from hostile 'savages,' starvation, and severe weather. Mere survival was the main social, political, and cultural interest on the early frontier. Several petitions originated along the frontier calling for fully independent, autonomous countries to be formed. Areas which were then part of Virginia, Pennsylvania, New York, and New Hampshire petitioned those state governments to become independent, self-governed areas. To really appreciate the difficulty involved here, we must remember that, at the time, Virginia, for example, extended all the way to the Mississippi.

The same objections and arguments which the colonists had used against George III and England to justify the American Revolution were now turned against the federal government of the United States and against the individual state governments (all located in eastern cities naturally) by those living on the frontier. The federal government was unfair and ineffective they claimed. It was too distant (geographically) from and insensitive and unresponsive (politically) to the frontier and the needs and concerns of the people living on the frontier. At the same time, more and more people were 'moving West'—going into the unsettled, frontier lands to seek their fortunes (or, at least, to find their places) in the New World.

The First Federal Tax on Whiskey

During this same period, the federal government and the individual states were in trouble financially. Alexander Hamilton, Secretary of the Treasury, was a strong federalist who supported the authority and power of the federal government over the authority of the individual states. Ironically, Hamilton managed to strengthen the authority of the central federal government by proposing that the federal government take over responsibility for the financial debts which the individual states had incurred during the Revolution. After all, *before* the Revolution there was no federal government and no federal funds to be used to wage the war against England. Such a proposal would strengthen the hand of the federal government by strengthening the power of the federal government to raise taxes and, by adopting the debts of the individual states, Hamilton cleverly managed to guarantee the support of the states for a more powerful central government. Hamilton won the support of both President George Washington and Congress for his proposal, and, in March, 1791, the first federal excise tax became the law of the land.

Now what does all of this have to do with whiskey? Well, once all of the philosophical debates about federal authority and states rights were concluded and once all of the political maneuvering was finished and the deals were cut, and once things came down to the practical matter of where the money was to come from and what was to be the source of the revenue, the practiced eye of the politicians landed upon whiskey. The first Federal Excise Bill of 1791 was a federal excise tax on whiskey and whiskey stills.

There are some very important things to be noticed about the fact that whiskey was considered to be the best source of revenue for the federal government during the first real budgetary crisis of this country. One of the things this tells us is how important whiskey was at the time and what a tremendously large sum of money was involved. This was a time when there were several thousand known commercial stills operating in the western parts of Pennsylvania, Virginia, and North Carolina, and when, additionally, practically every farmer and settler had a small still. That Washington, Hamilton, and the United States Congress considered whiskey to be the most likely source of the millions of dollars of desired revenue tells us a great deal about the importance of whiskey at the time.

The enactment of the Federal Excise tax is also a very good early example of the exercise of political influence. The excise tax on whiskey fell particularly heavily upon the under-represented and politically impotent people along the frontier since much of their trade was just that—trade or barter. On the frontier, very little actual money ever changed hands. Whiskey was bartered for dry goods, or horses, or even land. There was little or no source of money income on the frontier to be used to pay a tax. Those who produced whiskey which could be transported to the eastern cities where it could be marketed for actual cash could easily accommodate the tax by simply passing on the increase to the consumer—the beginning of what has since become a fine, American tradition. Thus, for the people living in the western lands the 1791 Federal Excise Tax on whiskey was an exercise in gross insensitivity and an example of the kind of unfair taxation which had helped to precipitate the break of the colonies from England. This taxation of whiskey set the stage for the first major test of the sovereignty of the union and the first major threat of possible armed revolt against the federal government of the United States—what has become known as the Whiskey Rebellion.

Violence on the Frontier

The reception given to the official tax collectors who were sent to collect the whiskey tax was hostile, and the physical and practical business of collecting the tax was a nightmare for these collectors. They had actually to go onto private land to locate the stills, determine their production capacity, and estimate the quantity of whisky produced by each one. A series of incidents involving violence spread along the frontier—particularly in western Pennsylvania and what

was later to become Kentucky. Tax collectors were beaten and occasionally tarred, feathered, and run out of town by 'the whiskey
boys.' In one of the more serious and more highly publicized incidents in the summer of 1794, the home of John Neville in western
Pennsylvania was attacked by an armed group of men. Neville had
been a prominent citizen, but he became an 'exciseman' and was
particularly diligent and aggressive about enforcing the tax. Neville
and his home, known as Bower Hill, were defended by a group of
soldiers from Fort Fayette in Pittsburgh. A two-day battle ensued,
and although the reports of casualties varied, at least several men
were killed or seriously wounded. Included among the fatalities were
at least one regular soldier from Fort Fayette, and, on the side of
the whiskey 'revolutionaries,' Major James McFarlane, a popular
local veteran and hero of the Revolutionary War. Following the fu-
neral of the popular McFarlane, the seriousness of the crisis wors-
ened. The United Sates mail carriers were robbed, and a group of
what was estimated at 7,000 armed militia and local citizens gathered on August 1st just outside Pittsburgh and threatened to seize
and occupy the town.

The Watermelon Army

Although the crowd of 'whiskey soldiers' eventually dispersed with
no reported injury to person or property, this threat of violence was
the last straw for President Washington. While the situation with
the 'whiskey rebellion' was by far the most serious, Washington was
faced at the same time with several other challenges to federal authority in Pennsylvania, Georgia, and Kentucky (which had become
the 15th state on June lst, 1792). Washington felt the need for a
strong response and a show of federal force to bolster the authority
of the United States government. The Supreme Court issued an official proclamation that the actions of the whiskey soldiers in western Pennsylvania constituted an act of armed rebellion against the
union, and Washington issued a call for troops to the governors of
the states. Meanwhile, reports of violence from the frontier, particularly western Pennsylvania continued to spread. By the end of
September, Washington had assembled a force of nearly 3,000 men

from the state militias of Delaware, Maryland, New Jersey, North
Carolina, and Pennsylvania. These forces were under the command
of 'Light Horse' Harry Lee, a Virginian and the father of Robert E.
Lee. Washington joined the army and marched for Carlisle, Pennsylvania, the site of a recent meeting protesting the excise tax.

As Washington continued westward with his show of military
force, the ranks of what was to become known as the 'Watermelon
Army' grew. This was a pejorative name given to the men of the
various state militias by those who sympathized with the members
of the rebellion. This 'army' was a rag-tag bunch of civilians with
poor discipline and doubtful military abilities. The Watermelon
Army marched to Bedford and Shippensburg, on to Berkeley
Springs, West Virginia, and then on to Cumberland, Maryland, by
which time the forces had grown to approximately 15,000—a larger
contingent of troops than had ever been assembled for any of the
engagements of the Revolutionary War itself.

Washington's show of force served its intended purpose. There
was no armed resistance from any of the would-be whiskey soldiers or protesters of the excise tax, and Washington soon returned
to Philadelphia having effectively crushed the threat to the federal
government. While some of the leaders of the whiskey rebellion
were sought out and arrested and some of the troops were garri-
soned in western Pennsylvania for the winter, there were no more
serious outbreaks of resistance to the excise tax on whiskey, and
the Whiskey Rebellion was ended. Many of the angry, frustrated,
and disenchanted supporters of the Whiskey Rebellion left western
Pennsylvania and moved down the Ohio River into what was to
become northern and central Kentucky and southern Ohio. Early
historians of the period have indicated that the Whiskey Rebellion
constituted a serious threat to the preservation of the republic and
have credited Washington's decisive actions as crucial at what was
a pivotal point in the life of the country which he had played such a
major role in creating.

Whiskey and the Civil War

Both the population of the United States and the demand for whiskey boomed during the mid-1800s, and the average per capita

consumption continued to rise steadily. When the time came to recruit soldiers from both North and South for the Civil War, the role played by whiskey was an important one despite the efforts of the Prohibition organizations. Whiskey rations had been a part of the life of a soldier in the army of the United States since its beginning. We know that whiskey helped see George Washington and his troops through the bitter winters of 1777 and 1778 in Valley Forge. Beginning in the early 1800s, whiskey rations were officially supplied by government contractors through the War Department. The daily ration was usually one gill—a fourth of a pint. Although the official, regular ration of whiskey for members of the United States Army ended in 1830, whiskey had remained an integral part of life in the military. Officers still had the authority to provide whiskey to those in their command as 'special issue' which, given the extreme conditions which existed much of the time, occurred quite frequently.

Most officers simply ignored the high incidence of 'unofficial' use of alcohol among the troops. Remember, this was at a time when alternative beverages were very few and when large supplies of safe, fresh water were relatively scarce. It is no accident that many of the major battles of the Civil War were fought near rivers, streams, and creeks. Just as modern armies depend upon petroleum fuels, the armies of the nineteenth century were dependent upon water. This was also a period when the medicinal effects of alcohol were greatly exaggerated. In addition to the normal, medical uses of whiskey to treat various aliments, it was used as both an antiseptic and anesthetic.

Perhaps one of the best-known stories concerning whiskey comes from the Civil War. In 1864, Ulysses S. Grant was named by Lincoln to command all Union forces and he was to receive credit for finally bringing an end to the war. Of course, it was Grant who accepted Robert E. Lee's surrender at Appomattox Courthouse in 1865. Earlier in the war in 1862, however, when the North still expected a quick and easy victory, Grant was bitterly attacked by critics and accused of mismanagement because of the high number of Union casualties at the Battle of Shiloh. Members of Congress and several Northern newspapers publicly attacked Grant and asked President

Lincoln to replace him. As part of this attack, Grant was accused of drinking too heavily. However, Lincoln was extremely supportive of Grant since Grant was willing to take the initiative to actually engage the Confederates at a time when other Union commanders were avoiding engagements. In a response which has now become well-known, Lincoln said, "I can't spare this man—he fights . . . ." It was also reported but later denied by Lincoln that he added, "I wish I knew what brand of whiskey he drinks. I would send a barrel to all my other generals."

The Whiskey Ring

The close connection with whiskey was to follow Grant after the war and during his tenure as President of the United States; however, the connection this time was, in fact, a scandalous one. Now political scandal seems to have been a regular feature of American life since the very beginning of the country. Most recent and most prominent of these are the scandals involving Watergate during the Nixon administration and the Savings and Loan and Iran-Contra scandals of the Reagan administration. Perhaps the most notable political scandal of modern times was the Teapot Dome scandal of 1923 during the administration of Warren Harding. So, we have had scandals which were precipitated by fraud involving oil leases on federal lands, the illegal sale of military arms, political elections and 'dirty tricks,' banking, and real estate.

Not to be outdone, the whiskey industry has had its very own scandal—and of major proportions. During the early 1870s under the administration of Grant following the War Between the States, several major members of Grant's administration were implicated in a major scandal involving whiskey fraud. This group, which included Orville Babcock, Grant's Secretary, William Avery, Chief Clerk of the Internal Revenue Service, and John McDonald, a district tax collector supervisor appointed by Grant, became known as the Whiskey Ring. At the time, the whiskey industry was operating under strict federal guidelines and supervision. The production of distilleries was monitored to ensure that the distilleries paid the appropriate taxes on the amount of whiskey produced. The Ring operated simply by allowing the distilleries to operate and produce more whiskey than was reported for tax purposes. The distilleries were thus allowed to save whatever dollars would have otherwise been spent on taxes—which ran into the millions of dollars. Such fraud was made possible by running the distilleries after hours, by keeping duplicate sets of books, by dumping barrels of whiskey without the proper 'dumping notice' required by law, and, of course, by numerous and generous bribes of various government officials both low and high. Although rumors had circulated for years, the scandal finally was broken open in 1875 when a 'sting operation' resulted in the arrest and prosecution of the major figures in the Whiskey Ring.

The White House and the Whiskey Ring

A series of bizarre events (which certainly rival anything which Watergate or Iran-Contra have had to offer) were set into motion by the investigation and resulting trials involving members of the Whiskey Ring. During the trial, Grant, in a move typical of his fumbling ineptitude as president, publicly announced that he intended to testify for the defense in a criminal trial being prosecuted by his own Department of Justice. In a move similar to Reagan's videotaped testimony in the Iran-Contra trial, Grant testified by deposition rather than in the open courtroom in St. Louis. His avid defense of Babcock along with several legal blunders and personnel changes within the prosecution resulted in Babcock's acquittal and the general suspicion that others in Grant's administration (and possibly even Grant himself) were involved. In an ironic move, Babcock was thereafter named by Grant to become Inspector of Lighthouses. McDonald was convicted but received a minimum sentence and set a pattern which was to be followed by other figures in major political scandals (such as Gordon Liddy and Oliver North) by writing a book about his exploits in which he implicated Grant in the Whiskey Ring. The attacks upon Grant in McDonald's book, entitled *Secrets of the Great Whiskey Ring*, published in 1880, as well as other scandals involving members of Grant's administrations (including the better known 'Gold Scandal' and scandals involving Indian affairs and the railroads), and the well-known fact that Grant had accepted expensive and lavish personal gifts, effectively ended Grant's political career. When some members of the Republican Party tried to nominate Grant for a third term in 1880, after the intervening administration of Rutherford B. Hayes, the Convention chose James Garfield instead, and Grant slipped from public life with the lingering odor of scandal and whiskey fraud still wafting from the historical accounts of his administrations.

The Whiskey Trust

When the subject of test cases concerning monopolies and antitrust measures is raised, everyone initially thinks of the famous case of the Standard Oil Company. However, whiskey is certainly every bit as American as oil, and the whiskey industry established its own Whiskey Trust in an attempt to control the whiskey trade just as Standard Oil did in an attempt to control the oil trade. In the late 1880s and early 1890s the whiskey industry operated under a trust agreement, copied from the agreement used by Standard Oil. The establishment of this Whiskey Trust, with the official name of the Distillers' and Cattle Feeders' Trust, headquartered in Peoria, Illinois, gave control of independent companies (and supposedly, competitors) to a single group of 'trustees' who then operated the combined trust as if it were a single company. Prices could be raised or lowered in different markets to compel independent distillers to join the trust or be forced out of business.

The Whiskey Trust was the source of a great amount of turmoil both within the whiskey industry and between the whiskey industry and the general public. For the most part the Whiskey Trust controlled the manufacture and marketing of neutral spirits—unaged, colorless, odorless, and flavorless spirits produced more economically at higher proofs and used in making cheaper, blended whiskeys. Thus, a tension was created between the distilleries represented by the trust and the distilleries which produced and marketed aged, straight Bourbon with the former located, for the most part, in Illinois, Indiana, and Ohio, and the latter grouped in Kentucky, Pennsylvania, Maryland, and Tennessee, with the Ohio River forming the boundary. Market control, price fixing, and alleged brib-ery and violence by the trust further alienated the whiskey people not affiliated with the trust. By the mid-1890s, there was also grow-ing dissatisfaction of the general public as a result of the continu-ous pattern of political bribery, scandal, and price controls and kick-backs. Just how influential the strong negative public sentiment was in the formation of the Prohibition Party and in the eventual passage of the Eighteenth Amendment to the United States Consti-tution which established Prohibition on January 16th, 1919, is dif-ficult to say. However, even before federal prohibition, a large num-ber of individual states had already decided to become 'dry.'

There were congressional investigations into the trust during the 1890s, and anti-trust legislation was passed. During the investi-gations, the Whiskey Trust went through several dissolutions and re-namings, leaving a complicated legal trail for investigators to follow. During Prohibition, the National Distillers Products Corpo-ration, a direct descendent of the old Distillers' and Cattle Feeders' Trust, bought stores of high-quality aging Bourbon in bonded ware-houses, and following the repeal of Prohibition, National Distillers became the largest company in the American whiskey industry. Thus, ironically, the distilleries north of the Ohio River, which produced the blended whiskeys and which originally formed the Whiskey Trust, are now out of business, and the distilleries south of the Ohio River which produced the aged, straight Bourbon survived the chal-lenge of the Whiskey Trust only to see National Distillers become the leading company in the industry following Prohibition.

Just before the Civil War, temperance organizations began to form in various states and cities. It is interesting that it took so long for any organized opposition to alcohol to develop in the United States since, as we have seen, the consumption of alcohol and the making of whiskey had been a part of American life since the very beginning of the Colonies. There are several reasons why the Tem-perance Movement began in the mid-nineteenth century. Perhaps the single most important one was the dramatic increase in per capita alcohol consumption. From the time of the American Revo-lution to approximately 1830, the per capita consumption rate of distilled spirits had increased from about two gallons per person to over five gallons per person annually! This means an average of over five gallons for every man, woman, and child in the general population, drinker and non-drinker alike, so; the actual average consumption of adults drinkers was, by present-day standards, astronomical. While accurate figures are hard to verify, there was undoubtedly widespread abuse. The American Temperance Society once estimated that half of the men were consuming two-thirds of all of the whiskey consumed.

Water, Water Everywhere

There is no evidence, in the records, of any serious opposition to the consumption of alcohol from the earliest colonial times to the 1830s. Part of the reason for this lack of opposition must lie in an answer to the question what *else* (besides alcoholic beverages) did people drink? The most popular drink of the early colonists was cider—usually hard (alcoholic) apple cider, a drink which was to remain the country's favorite until the late nineteenth century, when many farmers destroyed their apple orchards as a result of over-zealous temperance fervor. The second most popular drink from the mid-sixteenth century until about 1800 was rum. Rum was replaced by Bourbon and rye whiskeys. Contrary to some popular beliefs, consumption of beer and wine in early America was very low. But what about the non-drinkers? What else was there to drink? There were no soft drinks and no fresh citrus juices. What about water? Well, there was plenty of water around but very little potable water. The technology was not available to dig deep wells and the shallow surface water was frequently deadly, the source of 'swamp fever.' Fresh water was available from rivers and lakes, but the only means available to purify such water was sedimentation, a slow and ineffective process. Ironically, an abundance of fresh, underground water was both a blessing and a curse. In Kentucky, for example, one reason that typhus and cholera spread so quickly was that the plentiful limestone water basin could easily be contaminated by body waste and then spread over a wide area. Mountain springs were the best source of fresh, potable water, but these were not accessible to most people. Cisterns which gathered rainwater also were in common use, but there was simply not enough safe, fresh water, especially for travellers and city-dwellers. It begins to make sense then why so many people drank so much whiskey whose alcohol content was also a guarantee of its antiseptic quality.

Booz Bottles

Of course, when fresh water was available, it had to be transported from its source to where it was to be used, and fresh water did not stay fresh very long. The availability of containers other than wooden barrels, which were themselves often the source of contamination, was very limited. Before about 1820 glass jugs, bottles, and flasks were rare and prized possessions. When glass bottles did become widely available in the 1820s and 1830s as a result of mass production the main demand came from the whiskey industry which used glass containers to promote its own products. Hundreds of glass companies became involved in the business of making whiskey bottles. This was the origin of decorative decanters, and yes, one of the most popular designs which dates from 1840, in the shape of a

Stoneware jugs, typical whiskey containers prior to glass bottles

From the Oscar Getz Museum collection

small house, was produced by a distiller in Philadelphia by the name of E.C. Booz. 'Booze' is an old word derived from the Middle English 'bousen' and the Middle Dutch word 'busen' which mean 'to carouse.' When the bottles designed by Mr. Booz became so popular, the word 'booze' was also popularized and indelibly linked in the public's eye with the whiskey itself.

These Booz Bottles were actually owned by individuals or by the barkeepers or saloons since whiskey was still commonly sold, in bulk, in barrels. A.M. Bininger and Company was one of the earliest distillers to sell whiskey in glass bottles. The oldest known bottle with 'Bourbon' on the label is a Bininger bottle which dates to 1849. For the most part, distillers did not begin to market their products in bottles in mass quantity until after the Civil War. 'Old Forester' Kentucky Bourbon, named after the Confederate hero, Nathan Bedford Forrest, and made in Marion County, was the first whiskey to be marketed from the rectifier solely in sealed, glass bottles under its own label—not in bulk (Old Forester was a blend until Prohibition).

The alcohol content of cider and whiskey killed whatever contamination there might have been and prevented fresh contamination. The persistent myth of the alleged medicinal benefits of drinking whiskey, which lasted into the early part of the twentieth century, probably arose from the relative benefits of whiskey over water since the whiskey was contaminant-free. The rise of the temperance movement followed the industrial revolution with its technology for digging deep wells to produce large quantities of fresh water for cities.

The Rise of the Temperance Movement

Small societies opposing the public use of alcohol date from the late part of the eighteenth century when the first recorded temperance society was organized in Litchfield County, Connecticut, in 1789. Other scattered efforts followed in the first part of the nineteenth century including the New York State Temperance Society, started in 1828, and the Congressional Temperance Society, started in Washington, D.C., in 1833. The first temperance group to organize an attempt to attract a national membership and to have members sign pledges of complete abstinence from the use of alcohol was a group called the Washingtonians. Founded in 1840, by mid-century the group claimed a membership of a half million! The Sons of Temperance was another very popular national temperance organization during the 1840s and 1850s, with chapters in several different states.

Opposition to the use of alcohol was clearly growing by the mid-nineteenth century. In the next few decades, the high per capita consumption rate, the scandals surrounding The Whiskey Ring and The Whiskey Trust, and the desire for more productive workers raised by the beginning of the Industrial Revolution, all served to create a negative public attitude toward the manufacture, distribution, and consumption of whiskey. The temperance movement gained momentum and strength in the period following the Civil War. In 1869, the National Prohibition Party was organized. Ohio was to take the lead in the temperance movement. In 1874, the Women's Christian Temperance Union, which was soon to become recognized (and feared, by many) by its initials, W.C.T.U., was organized there. Encouraged by the success of the W.C.T.U., male opponents to the use of alcohol organized another powerful and very effective group in Ohio in 1893, known as the Anti-Saloon League. Crusaders for the W.C.T.U. and the Anti-Saloon League were scattered across the country. Armed with books and pamphlets describing the evils of drinking alcohol in any form, these crusaders spoke to civic, church, and school groups urging people to sign 'The Pledge' to completely abstain from drinking any form of alcohol and to vote for 'local options laws' which gave towns and counties the option of going 'dry,' prohibiting the sale or consumption of all alcoholic beverages. By one of those strange quirks which defies logic but which frequently occurs in the course of human affairs, 'temperance' (moderate use) had now come to mean 'abstinence.' The struggle which was to culminate in national Prohibition had begun.

Carry Nation

Social movements are usually most effective when led by a single dynamic and charismatic leader. Carry Nation proved to be such a leader for the temperance movement. By 1899, when she began to wield her sledge hammers and her now infamous hatchet, 'temperance' had come to mean prohibition. The opposition of 'temperance' groups was no longer just to the immoderate use of alcohol but rather to the use of any alcohol whatsoever. By this time American-made whiskey—including some rye whiskey but primarily Bourbon whiskey—had displaced rum as America's drink of choice so it was Bourbon which was the primary target of Carry Nation, the W.C.T.U., and the other temperance groups.

Nation claimed to be in direct communication with God and to be instructed by God to attack the places of devil worship, the saloons and the 'demons' who worshipped there. She began her campaign in 1899 in Medicine Lodge, Kansas, where she lived with her second husband, a Protestant minister, and soon thereafter enlarged her campaign in highly publicized attacks on saloons in Kiowa and Wichita. Joined by other women who were members of the W.C.T.U., Nation swept across Kansas wrecking and destroying saloons with rocks and sledgehammers and her signature hatchet, often praying and singing hymns while in the process.

Feelings ran very strong about the issues of saloons and alcohol, and Nation certainly further polarized the sides. There seemed to be no middle ground, no compromise position concerning the consumption of alcohol—you were either for it or against it. There were bitter fights between members of the anti-saloon groups and those defending the saloons. Churches as well as saloons were attacked. Shots were fired and people injured in several fights (though there were no reported deaths). Nation herself was attacked and beaten. Her speeches were often greeted by many people with taunts, curses, rotten eggs, and rotten vegetables and by others with praise, prayers, and hymns. She was jailed several times and threatened with horse-whipping and being tarred and feathered. Like many other zealots, Carry, whether divine-guided or mis-guided, showed great courage and persisted in her attacks. She captured the imagination of the country, and her exploits were often front page, headline news in major newspapers across the country. She enlarged her campaign to attack sex and tobacco as well as alcohol. It was the country's first (and perhaps only) major morals crusade. Nation's crusade against saloons and alcohol spread across the Midwest to the West Coast, and later to New York City. She even travelled to England and Scotland to lecture against the evils of whiskey where her reception was anything but friendly and her efforts anything but successful.

Nation continued her campaign of speeches and saloon-smashing until her death in 1911, the result of a stroke she is said to have suffered while leading a particularly rousing effort against saloons in Eureka Springs, Missouri. While Nation was certainly not alone in her opposition to saloons and alcohol and while she was not even the first to physically attack saloons with rocks and hatchets, she certainly coalesced and solidified the anti-saloon and anti-alcohol forces. Nation became one of the country's first major figures recognized as a social reformer, and what had been scattered opposition to saloons and the beer and spirits industries became the Temperance Movement. From here the road to national Prohibition was a short and wide one.

Saloon Life

Much of the Temperance Movement was aimed not only at the consumption of alcohol but at the particular social institution which had grown up around the sale and consumption of alcohol—the saloon. Saloons were a major social institution in the larger cities in the United States from the end of the Civil War until the beginning of Prohibition in 1920, figuring prominently in the political, social, and sporting life of the country. However, there was a great deal about saloon life which many people disliked, so many who tolerated the sale and consumption of beer and whiskey nonetheless opposed the life which had developed around the saloons.

The dramatic rise in the number and popularity of saloons in the early nineteenth century probably resulted, to a large extent, from the increasing numbers of immigrants—particularly Germans and Irish. There was a wide variety of saloons, in both style and quality. At one end of the scale was the 'barrel house,' which primarily sold rectified whiskey—inferior high-proof neutral spirits flavored with straight Bourbon (see Chapter 2). Racks of barrels of whiskey lined the walls where the sales were made directly into the customers' containers by bulk (usually a gallon at a time). Individual drinks were also drawn directly from the barrels. This was cut-rate, 'rot-gut' whiskey sold with little or no niceties or embellishments. Sawdust covered the floors. Furnishings were sparse. There was none of the fancy trimmings associated with 'higher class' saloons. Located in the larger cities, these 'fancy' saloons represented a completely different world. They were gathering places which attracted the rich and famous of the day by their lavish designs and furnishings—the forerunners of the excessive opulence of today's Las Vegas. Crystal chandeliers lighted the original 'saloon art' hung behind the bar or on the walls—reproductions or original oil paintings of well-endowed, Rubenesque nudes in classical guise. Famous examples included 'Venus in the Bath,' 'Diana Surprised,' and 'Cleopatra at the Bath.' An entire art industry was built around providing these works of art for saloons. Sporting figures also were common subjects for saloon art. John L. Sullivan, heavyweight boxing champion of the world from 1882 to 1892, was a favorite as was 'Gentleman Jim' Corbett, who won the title from Sullivan in 1892. This might have been the only opportunity for many people to see what their hero actually looked like.

The Free Lunch

A common and very popular feature of the saloons was the free lunch. It is difficult to determine exactly where the practice of offering free lunches in saloons began, but the two cities that have the strongest claim to originating the practice—New Orleans and San Francisco—are still today identified with fine food. The spreads provided were lavish, and the different saloons in the major cities tried to outdo one another in the exquisite gastronomical delights they offered. Ethnic saloons offered ethnic foods. For example, popular German saloons offered knockwurst, bologna, pickles, onions, and rye bread. But, as the familiar saying now records, 'There ain't no such thing as a free lunch.' The free lunches, of course, were merely attractions to get customers into the saloons, and 'freeloaders' were not tolerated. The customary procedure called for the customers to buy at least one or two drinks of whiskey before proceeding to the table with the food. The standard drink had now become Bourbon, but rye whiskey was also still in demand. Knowledgeable drinkers preferred straight whiskey and avoided the blended whiskey, the result of combining neutral spirits with some straight Bourbon (see Chapter 2 below). Successful saloons did not lose money by offering free lunches. The lunches were simply one of the early marketing gimmicks used by businesses in America. Customers would spend several hours a day in the saloons and saloons were frequently 'full service' institutions providing baths, private rooms, 'indoor' plumbing facilities, cigars, and entertainment, including gambling. The added attraction of free food was profitable to the saloons.

There Is No Free Lunch

For some period of time, saloons were quite respectable places attracting not only national figures—politicians, entertainers and athletes—but local notaries as well. By the turn of the twentieth century, though, things had begun to turn dark for the saloons and for the social life centered on them. As we have seen, saloons, not distilleries, were the main targets of Carry Nation and other temperance crusaders. Things were also changing dramatically in American society; there was increasing competition for the public's time and money—not only amongst the saloons themselves—but from the silent movies and from the opportunities offered by the automobile. The way the saloons were structured, they depended upon the steady trade of regular customers who would spend quite some period of time each day in the saloons. New occupations and opportunities for travel threatened the regular clientele as well as did regulatory legislation aimed at controlling and limiting the number of saloons. British investors bought breweries, and following a practice still common in England, chains of saloons became attached to certain breweries or distilleries or wholesalers, selling products only from that brewery or distillery or wholesale warehouse. When the owners of different chains of saloons tried to buy political favor for their own saloons and political disfavor for their competitors, widespread political graft and corruption in several major cities, including now infamous cases involving New York and San Francisco, were the result. Saloons had come to attract prostitutes and other 'undesirables' such as unemployed, chronic drunkards. By the early part of the twentieth century, saloon life had begun to lose its grip on American social life. Various states put an end to saloon life by enacting state prohibition—some as early as 1910, and when national Prohibition became law in January 1920, saloon life passed permanently from the American scene.

Prohibition

As a result of the Eighteenth Amendment to the United States Constitution, national Prohibition became the law of the land at 12:01 A.M. on January 17th, 1920, and thus began one of the most colorful and puzzling periods of American history. An earlier attempt to pass the Eighteenth Amendment in 1914 had failed, but the Webb-Kenyon Act passed by Congress in 1913 had already made it illegal to transport whiskey from a 'wet' location to a 'dry' one. It was not only illegal to sell or drink whiskey in the locations in which it was made, but it was also illegal to buy it somewhere else and bring it back home. By 1920, as a result of what were known as 'local option laws,' many states had become dry. In some cases this process itself was very curious since several states became dry simply by a vote of the state legislatures without any public referendum or vote at all. These states included Alabama, Arkansas, Georgia, Idaho, Iowa, New Hampshire, Mississippi, Tennessee, Texas, and Utah. Of course, other states were dry by a vote of the general population and many counties and cities in other states were also dry as a result of local option laws. By 1919, a total of 31 states were already dry or had voted to become dry. So a lot of the country was already dry before the Eighteenth Amendment went into effect in 1920. A significant aspect of the process of the successful campaign by temperance groups using local option laws was the way in which temperance was tied to patriotism. Since the production of whiskey uses grain, and given the food shortages created during the First World War, using corn to make whiskey instead of food was viewed

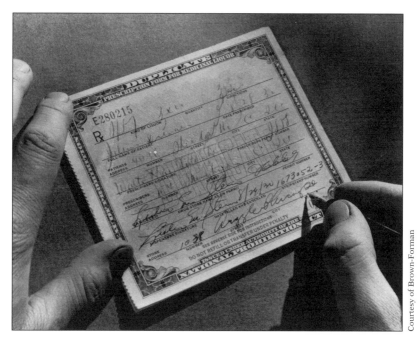

A Prohibition-era medical prescription for whiskey

by many people as 'un-American.' Indeed, two years before it passed the Eighteenth Amendment, Congress passed the Lever Food and Fuel Control Act to establish emergency measures during the war, and the use of any food products (including rye and corn) to make whiskey was expressly prohibited. National Prohibition was the end result of what some have estimated to be a fifty-year and $50 million campaign by the supporters of the temperance organizations. The successful culmination of the temperance movement remains a unique example in American history of what an expensive, high-pressure, grass-roots social movement can accomplish. The labor movement and the civil rights movement are the only other social movements which have approximated the success of the temperance movement.

Moonshine

What the supporters of temperance got, however, was not what they wanted or expected. Never, it seems, has the law of the land been so out of touch with the people of the land. The details of enforcing the Prohibition contained in the Eighteenth Amendment were contained in the Volstead Act which defined an alcoholic beverage as any beverage containing more than one-half of one percent alcohol. The continued manufacture, distribution, and sale of whiskey for medicinal purposes were still legal, and stores of aging whiskey in warehouses came under government control and protection.

The enforcement of the Volstead Act, the responsibility of the Internal Revenue Service, proved to be impossible. 'Old John Barleycorn,' the name used to symbolize whiskey in poetry and song, refused to die peacefully and to be buried. Across the country, widespread violation was common. The illegal manufacture, transportation, distribution and consumption of whiskey, known as bath-tub gin or moonshine, were rampant. Moonshine was known by many different names, many of them regional designations for illegal whiskey—moonshine, moon, white mule, white lightning, mountain dew, bootlegger whiskey, and corn squeezin's. The use of the word 'white' in names for whiskey is because the 'white dog,' whiskey straight out of the still before aging, is clear. This gave rise to the expression used to describe the use of a small amount of whiskey as a hangover remedy: 'the hair of the dog that bit you.'

Speakeasies and other private, illegal clubs where whiskey was consumed flourished. Illegal whiskey attracted criminals and resulted in one of the most violent periods in American history.

The revenue loss for the federal government from the legal manufacture and sale of whiskey was enormous. Some have estimated the tax loss to the Federal Treasury to have been as high as nearly $500 million a year. Local, city, and state governments also lost their share of legitimate taxes on legal whiskey. Of course, the racketeers and bootleggers did not pay any taxes. And, of course, the attempted enforcement by the Internal Revenue Service and Elliot Ness cost tax dollars.

The hidden costs of Prohibition were also enormous. For example, the market for corn, barley, and rye plummeted, literally overnight. Agriculture was turned upside down. Farmers converted millions of acres of land which had produced corn to the production of other grains—primarily wheat. The result was a glut on the market, a dramatic drop in prices, and financial ruin for many farmers. Tens of thousands of workers from the legal manufacture, transportation, distribution and sale of whiskey were put out of work. These included not just those who worked directly at the distilleries or for the distributors, but all of the related laborers as well—the farmers who supplied the grains to the distilleries, the workers at the plants which manufactured the glass bottles, the printers which made the labels for the bottles, the coopers who made the barrels, wholesale and retail sales staffs, advertising personnel, and workers in the rail and trucking industry involved with the transportation of everything from the raw grain to the finished product.

Scholars still argue over the details of exactly how Prohibition contributed to the Great Depression and the Stock Market Crash of 1929. There seems to be little room for doubt, however, that the loss of hundreds of millions of dollars of revenue for the Federal Treasury and the loss of tens of thousands of jobs contributed significantly to the Depression which swept across the country after 1929. Within a very brief period complete financial chaos resulted in the failure of thousands of businesses across the country. Thousands of banks across the country also failed. People lost everything they had in the banks, and tens of thousands of homes and farms were lost to foreclosure. The early 1930s were certainly one of the most difficult periods in America's history, and arguably, the victory of the temperance forces over the whiskey industry was a contributing factor.

In 1933, Franklin D. Roosevelt became President on the strength of his promise to lift the country out of the Depression. Part of the attempt to return the country to better times involved the repeal of the Eighteenth Amendment, accomplished by the Twenty-first Amendment. The end to Prohibition was the result of a long and bitter political battle which had raged for several years. The Association Against the Prohibition Amendment, headed by prominent businessman Pierre S. DuPont, was central in marshalling the pro-Repeal political and business forces. By 1932, both the Democratic and Republican parties as well as their candidates supported the move to repeal Prohibition.

Beer and wine sales became legal again on April 7th 1933, and Prohibition of whiskey was officially repealed on December 5th 1933, when Utah became the 36th state to ratify the Twenty-first Amendment, resulting in the necessary ratification by two-thirds of the states.

American Whiskey Following Repeal

When the end to Prohibition finally arrived, the legitimate American whiskey business in the United States was in a shambles. It had suffered through 14 years of national Prohibition but, as we have seen, many individual states had been dry for several years longer. Except for a few distilleries supplying 'medicinal' whiskey, the distilleries had been closed for at least 14 years. Equipment was ruined or obsolete. Trained and experienced labor was scarce. The network of people who supplied grains and bottles to the distilleries had become practically nonexistent. Supplies of high-quality, aged whiskey had dwindled. The intent of Prohibition was to destroy completely the whiskey business in America, and it had nearly succeeded. The recovery of the whiskey industry following Repeal was to be a long and difficult process. It was not until the 1950s that the industry fully recovered.

Prohibition had given organized crime a stranglehold on the whiskey business and a foothold in this country, and all the resources of the federal government had not been able to break those holds. Organized crime did not suddenly quit making and selling illicit whiskey, of course, simply because of Repeal. Competition now developed between legitimate and illicit whiskey for the consumer's dollar, and for some period of time, the illicit trade was better able to reach the customer. It already had the distilleries running, the supplies on hand, and the distribution network in place. The illicit trade did not have to worry about meeting all of the new federal and state laws and regulations which were put into place following Repeal. Since no taxes were paid on the illicit whiskey, it was also cheaper than whiskey made legally. Those involved in the illicit whiskey business merely had to worry about not getting caught by the authorities which, in comparison to the woes that now beset the legitimate whiskey business, seemed a rather minor worry.

Photograph by Mark Waymack

The tools of a nineteenth-century cooperage, as displayed at the Jim Beam Distillery

The Long Road Back

The road back by the American whiskey industry is a unique success story in the annals of American business. Following Repeal, American distillers were faced with a complicated and unprecedented maze of problems. National Prohibition had been lifted, but not all states had rescinded the earlier state legislative acts which had produced dry states. Even the 'wet' states had to pass legislation regulating the sale of whiskey, and there were unresolved legal issues involving federal taxes, state taxes, and licenses for distillers, wholesalers, and retailers. It took months for all of the necessary legal regulations to be put into place and then months longer for individuals to go through the maze of red tape to get the necessary licenses.

Meanwhile, imports of foreign-made whiskey became legal again also with few of the encumbering restrictions and regulations facing domestic made whiskeys. During Prohibition, Scotch and Canadian whiskies were regularly smuggled across the Canadian border. Americans in the northern United States, and particularly those in the large cities where the largest markets were, naturally developed a taste for these Scotch and Canadian whiskies. Not surprisingly then, when legal imports of foreign-made whiskey resumed immediately following Repeal, the Scotch and Canadian whiskies enjoyed an advantage over American whiskeys. Canada and Scotland had never suffered through Prohibition. It had meant a slight dip in their export market for a few years which had created good supplies of aged whiskey in their warehouses. The Canadian whisky industry thrived. Their distilleries were up and running and their workforce and distribution network were well-established. To export Canadian whisky to the United States involved the simple matter of driving their trucks across the border and paying the necessary taxes. Scotch whisky found its way to America in large quantities. Although national quotas were placed on the import of foreign-made whiskeys, the fact that relatively high-quality legal whiskeys became available to the American public almost immediately following Repeal was another tremendous problem for the American whiskey industry. American-made whiskey now had to compete with illicit domestic whiskey and legal foreign whiskey; so the first few years of resumed production of American whiskey were shaky. Even after everything was finally put back together again so that whiskey could actually be made, it still took several years of aging for the whiskey to mature in barrels to produce a quality product.

We doubt whether any other industry in the history of the United States was ever confronted by the obstacles which have faced the American whiskey industry.

The American whiskey industry has risen like a phoenix from the ashes of Prohibition and the daunting period following Repeal. Today, Kentucky Bourbon and Tennessee Sippin' Whiskey are recognized around the world as among the most sublime creations of human skill, tradition, and ingenuity. Most of this book is devoted to describing the best American whiskeys now available. But before we get to that, let's very briefly look at how whiskey is made—for this knowledge is essential to a full appreciation of the subtleties of American whiskey.

2

Making Whiskey

A warm breeze blows across the fields and up onto the hill where we sit, gazing out. Cumulus clouds, friendly cotton puffs earlier in the day, are piling up into the dark anvil shapes that threaten a thunderstorm. It is late summer. As we look down and across the open fields, we can see nearly everything necessary for the making of fine whiskey. Near the foot of the hill, a quiet spring gurgles into the open, forming a trickle that meets a small stream near the edge of the field. In the field itself the corn stands, tall stalks with full, ripe ears. Almost lost in the afternoon haze is a smaller field with another grain—perhaps barley or rye, we can't see for sure. And along two sides of the cornfield are massive stands of majestic oak trees. While it is yet too warm for an old-fashioned distillery to operate, the basic materials all lie at our feet.

The great whiskey distilleries are all located in the hilly country running from Virginia west through Kentucky and Tennessee. This is the happy result of the convergence of natural conditions particularly suited to the production of exceptional whiskey. The most important of these factors are: water, especially limestone water; grain, particularly corn; suitable oak for barrels; and climate, including warm summers and cool winters. In some ways by careful reckoning, and in some ways by lucky happenstance, people have learned over the centuries how to draw upon each of these crucial resources to make that wondrous elixir—American whiskey.

The Basic Ingredients

WATER

It all starts with water.

In our modern, largely urban era, we have become accustomed to generic municipal drinking water—water that has been collected, filtered, and chemically treated. Consuming several gallons of this clear liquid each day, we easily become lulled into the false notion that all water is the same.

From the chemist's point of view, pure water, plain old H_2O, is just that—plain water. Odorless, colorless, tasteless. But the chemist (and the good distiller) also knows that the water that we encounter in our everyday lives is certainly not pure H_2O. Often it is teeming with microscopic life—a quality that can sometimes disagree with the human digestive tract! But even when we find a water source free of such biological contaminants, there remains an incredible collection of other chemicals in small, but telling, quantities. These chemicals, largely minerals, change the way the water tastes as well as the way it reacts with other materials—as anyone who has tried to wash with soap in very hard water can readily attest. When it comes to water for drinking or for whiskey-making, purest is not best. The purest water, distilled water or clean rain water, lacks character. Character comes from minute quantities of naturally-occurring chemicals, mostly calcium salts.

Both because of the taste that it imparts and for the way it reacts with the grains in the distilling process, water rich in the minerals (especially calcium phosphate) leeched in its passage through limestone is particularly suited to making whiskey. Stories abound of legendary whiskey figures, such as Jacob Beam, Old Joe Peyton, or Jack Daniel, successfully prospecting for just the right 'limestone spring' from which to make their whiskey.

Water is crucial in a second way, a way in which it is not itself an 'ingredient.' As the warm alcoholic vapor makes its way from the still into the 'worm,' a reliable flow of cool water is required to course around the copper coil, condensing the vapor into whiskey (we shall say more about this later). Since it takes *cool* water to condense the distillate effectively, distilleries tend to shut down or greatly curtail operations during the warm summer months. And even with the technical feasibility of using artificially cooled condensers, the cost in the summer months would be prohibitive.

GRAIN

Grain is a fundamental building block of any whiskey. A good starchy grain is broken open and enzymes diligently convert the starch into fermentable sugars.

Traditional whiskies of Scotland and Ireland are made entirely from malted barley, though blended whiskies are predominantly grain alcohol—spirit distilled from a variety of grains. As farmers worked the fields of Virginia, Pennsylvania, Kentucky and Tennessee, they discovered that other grains provided better crop yields than barley. Rye tended to predominate in Pennsylvania, because

The basic building blocks of whiskey: corn, rye, and malted barley

Mark Waymack

of the rocky soil conditions and climate, whereas corn (maize) got the upper hand elsewhere. The use of these different grains in making whiskey gave rise to different styles of whiskey. And the federal government has over the years produced official definitions for such products as Bourbon, Tennessee Whiskey, rye whiskey, wheat whiskey, and corn whiskey.

The Process

MILLING

The process begins with corn being trucked into the distillery and unloaded from the truck. After being inspected for cleanliness and quality the grains are weighed and delivered to the mill. Here the corn is crushed into a coarse corn meal.

COOKING

Crushed into small bits, the corn is now unceremoniously dumped into a huge vat of hot water—and we mean *hot*. In this cooker it is brought up to the boiling point and cooked for a couple of hours. In some distilleries, this cooking is even done in huge pressure cookers, allowing for even higher temperatures and thereby getting a quicker cook as well as more complete rendering of the starchy cells. Other distillers proudly draw attention to their 'traditional,' open cookers, suggesting that while pressure cooking might perhaps increase yields slightly, it is a much too rough process on the corn grist, lowering the quality of the final product. Whichever method, here the cooking breaks down the tough cellular membranes of the corn cells, rendering the starch more accessible to enzymes that will be introduced in the mashing process.

After the corn grist has cooked sufficiently long, the temperature is allowed to fall. Then the rye is added to the cook.

MASHING

Since corn and unmalted rye are very low in enzymes (diastase and amylase are frequently used as interchangeable terms) enzyme-rich malted barley is crucial to the process. Once the rye (or occasionally wheat) has been cooked long enough, then the temperature is lowered yet again and the crushed malted barley is added. Typical proportions seem to run around 70–79 percent corn (though a few, such a Wild Turkey or the Jim Beam high rye formula, are lower than this), the remaining portion being split between malted barley and rye, though occasionally wheat is used—but there are trade secrets and variations are everywhere. Here in the soupy, warm porridge of the mash tub, the starch is converted by the enzymes into fermentable sugars—maltose and dextrins. For an efficient mash, the temperature must be kept between about 148 and 152 degrees Fahrenheit.

FERMENTING

Next the mash is pumped into the fermenting vats. In a commercial operation, these tubs are huge, ranging from 9,600 gallons to more than 50,000 gallons. Pour in the water from several backyard swimming pools, and you would still have room to spare. Traditionally these tubs were made of rot-resistant cypress. And while a few distilleries still make use of cypress fermenting tubs, they are the devil to maintain. Cleaning and sterilization are quite difficult. Hot water and steam are used, followed by a thick plaster of lime. And you can't ever let them really dry out, or the cypress boards will shrink somewhat, opening up leaks. Repairs take the skill of very talented, and increasing elusive craftsmen. Not surprisingly, nearly all of the distilleries have moved toward using stainless steel fermenting tubs.

Meeting the fresh mash in the fermenting tub is some of the leftover 'distiller's beer' from the last distillation. Called by many names—thin slop, backset, setback, yeast back—the proportion of this 'yeast back' tends to be around 25 percent of the total volume of the new mash. The high temperature of the distilling column has taken out the alcohol and killed the yeast, but the leftover spent beer is mildly acidic as a result of the fermentation process. Added to the new mash, the boost in acidity provided by the spent beer inhibits undesired bacteria and yeasts, making the mash—technically, but rarely by distillers, called 'wort' at this stage—safe for the desired distiller's yeast. It also provides a certain continuity in character between batches. It is from this step that we get the term,

Flowchart of the whiskey process

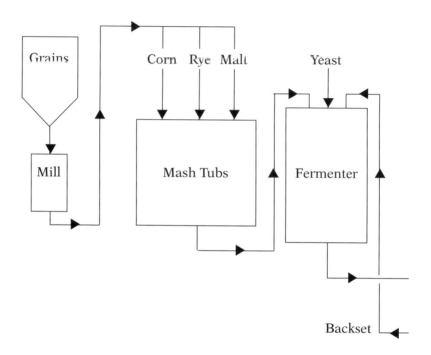

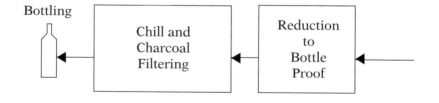

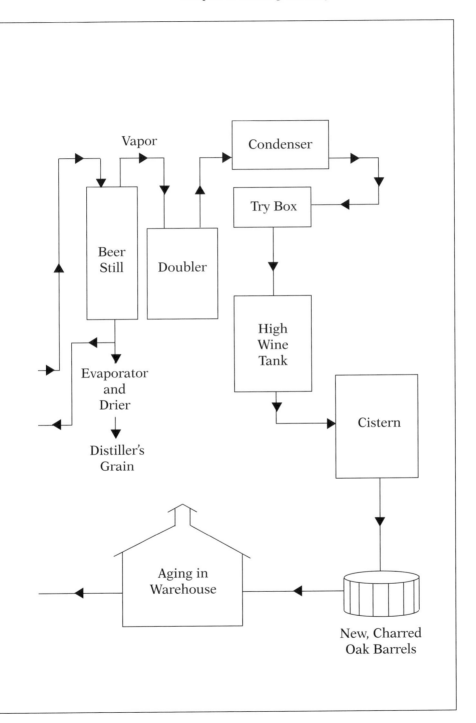

Vapor

Condenser

Try Box

Beer Still

Doubler

High Wine Tank

Evaporator and Drier

Distiller's Grain

Cistern

Aging in Warehouse

New, Charred Oak Barrels

'sour mash.' Because of the limestone character of the water, a sweet mash, that is, a mash not using any of the acidic 'yeast back,' would be pH neutral or even a bit alkaline, and hence at high risk of spoilage through undesired microbial growth. While the old timers might not have understood microbiological processes, they did understand that a sour mash would ferment with far more reliable and consistent results than a sweet mash.

The sour mash is cooled. In the old fashioned way, this is done by simply letting the air circulate around the tanks. In many modern plants, it is accomplished much more quickly by means of cooling coils inside the fermenters carrying cold water. These cooling coils not only serve to cool the mash at the beginning of the fermentation, they also help the distiller maintain an even temperature throughout the fermentation.

Meanwhile, under carefully controlled conditions, the distiller has been nurturing his yeast colony. Each distiller takes pride in his yeast culture, and carefully safeguards it to avoid contamination. In many cases, distillers speak with pride of their yeast culture which has been maintained through several generations, dating back to the end of Prohibition or even earlier. Different yeast strains do behave differently, leaving behind varying degrees of unfermented dextrins and other sugars. And these subtle differences in the fermentation can carry through into the final product: whiskey.

Small portions of yeast are taken from the mother culture and grown in the lab in progressively larger quantities over days and weeks, so that the distiller knows that when he has a mash ready he will have enough gallons of yeast to pitch in, ensuring a lively fermentation without bacterial infection.

Once the mash is cool enough, the distiller's yeast is pitched in to start the fermentation. In the fermentation process, the yeast digests the sugars produced in the mash, and as a by-product of digestion produces alcohol and carbon dioxide. The first day of the fermentation appears quiet, though the yeast is busy consuming sugar and propagating at an astonishing pace. By the second and third days, the vats become visibly active. At first small, fine bubbles form, then, as the fermentation accelerates the carbon dioxide bubbles raise the husky grains to the surface where they form a thick cap. Underneath, the liquid seems to seethe and boil. The

Pumping the mash into the fermenters at Maker's Mark

incessant fizzing sound of exploding bubbles fills the room. Indeed, the vigor of the ferment can actually produce a quite noticeable vibration in the vats. And then, as fermentation nears completion, the cap starts to break down, the bubbles get fewer, and larger and larger. As the last of the sugars are consumed by the yeast and converted into alcohol and carbon dioxide, a calmness returns to the wort.

DISTILLING

The crushed and cooked particles of corn are now swimming in a porridge which is about five percent alcohol—a close relative of beer. Indeed, this alcoholic soup is referred to as 'distiller's beer.' But this was never destined to be beer; whiskey is its future. So it is now pumped up and up, two to three storeys high, to the top of the column of the whiskey still.

In centuries past (and probably in illegal distilling today) the pot still was used—a copper pot with a copper worm coming out of its top. One pot of mash would be run at a time. The last of the commercial pot stills, however, were phased out of the American whiskey industry around 1900.

Today, American distillers make use of a column still, also known as a continuous still. Basically, the beer is pumped to the very top of the column, typically two to three storeys high. It enters the column at the top. From there gravity pulls it down through a multitude of baffle trays, called 'down comers,' designed to slow its progress. At the same time, steam is pumped in near the base of the column, from whence it rises, yielding its heat to the descending beer.

Experiments in making these columns from stainless steel, for the sake of economy in material and ease of cleaning, have not been successful. The traditional material, copper, has proven itself not only desirable because of its ability to exchange heat quite efficiently, but necessary because of certain chemical reactions with the beer. And in places where steel columns are used, they are now packed inside with all manner of copper items—copper screens, scrap copper pipe—to provide for chemical reactions necessary for a desirable whiskey.

The basic principle of distillation is quite straightforward. The boiling point of alcohol is 173–176 degrees Fahrenheit (there are different kinds of alcohols), whereas that of water is 212 degrees Fahrenheit. Thus, when the beer is heated, the alcohol boils off into vapor before the water. Now, a chemist could carefully control the temperature of the wort so that the distillate was very nearly pure alcohol. But pure alcohol has very little taste. It is pretty much a one-dimensional drinking experience. Hence, the whiskey-maker manages the distillation so that a certain measure of flavoring chemicals, called congeners, are carried through into the distillate. Too few of these trace components yields a whiskey devoid of taste and interest; too many of them produces a whiskey with an overabundance of impurities, heavy with fusel oils and aldehydes, laced with harsh flavors, prone to cause headaches and other undesirable results. Thus, one of the crucial skills of the master distiller is knowing how to manage this distillation process. In the old days of pot stills, the master distiller would reject the 'first shots' out of the still as too high in volatile chemicals; and he would reject the feints, or 'tailings,' as too high in water. He knew where the 'heart' of the distillation run was, and this is what he used to make the best whiskey. The control process is a bit different in a modern column still: it's possible to measure what used to be guessed at. How hot is the

Jimmy Russell surveying the fermenting mash at Wild Turkey

steam entering the bottom of the still? How much steam is entering? How hot are the vapors at the head of the column? By controlling these factors, the modern master distiller may ensure a first rate product.

While the porridge-like beer slowly works its way down the column, steam that has been forced in near the bottom rises through the column. As the hot steam rises it yields its heat to the descending beer, raising the temperature enough so that the alcohol evaporates. By the time it reaches the top of the column, the steam has cooled to about 185 degrees Fahrenheit and in the process has exchanged much of its water vapor for alcohol vapor.

This vapor now enters the cooling worm, traditionally a long coil of copper tubing. Cool water, taken from a nearby stream or pond, flows around the worm, cooling the vapor inside into an alcoholic liquid. After the first run, the alcoholic content has risen from 5 percent alcohol in the beer to around 55–60 percent alcohol in the distillate.

These 'low wines' are then put through the 'doubler,' a second quasi-distillation process that increases the alcoholic content to around 62–65 percent. By law, whiskey (other than neutral spirits) must come out of the still at less than 80 percent alcohol. But in practice, the norm is much lower than that, for the higher proof would yield a very thin, bland whiskey.

Several years ago, many distilleries tried to do away with the doublers, bringing the spirit off the column still at final proof, around 125–130 proof, which is 62.5–65 percent. But this produced a whiskey that still had certain undesirable impurities in it. So, in a fairly short time, the distillers were hustling about to rebuild their doublers. Happily, the doubler is once again a standard part of the distilling process.

The grain that we started with has now been transformed into an alcoholic spirit, but the process is far from complete. The fresh spirit, 'white dog,' is hardly something you would want to drink on a regular or social basis. Straight out of the still, it still has a cereal taste, with corn being particularly noticeable. A few distilleries employ various kinds of filtering at this stage. But in any case, the white dog is pumped into a cistern, where it is held until there is enough to load into barrels.

The leftover grain, a waste product in terms of whiskey, is yet valuable. A certain portion of the liquid in the spent beer, known commonly as the 'thin slop,' is returned to the fermenters as the yeast back. The 'thick slop,' however, is dried to about 10 percent moisture and sold as feed for cattle and horses. This feed, known as distillers' grain, is quite high in protein (since most of the starch has been converted and used in the whiskey-making), and is reputed to increase milk production in cows, weight gain in cattle, and strength in horses.

AGING

In the cistern, the whiskey is cut with pure water to bring it down to around 120–125 proof, i.e. 60–62.5 percent alcohol. It then goes into white oak barrels, with the finest of whiskeys—Bourbon and Tennessee Whiskey—going into new, white oak, charred barrels. (Corn whiskey, most closely identified with illegal 'moonshine,' tends not to be aged for very long, if at all. Other whiskeys, however, benefit enormously by maturation in oak barrels. Bourbon and Tennessee Whiskey, by law, must be aged at least two years in new, white oak, charred barrels.)

American White Oak, *Quercus alba,* is the wood of choice. Its strength, flexibility (so that the barrel staves may be bent to shape), its relative lack of porosity (so that not too much of the whiskey evaporates), and the chemical compounds that it offers for interaction with the new whiskey, make this wood the ideal candidate for barrel-making. Oak for barrel-making in America is mostly taken from Kentucky, Arkansas, and Missouri. The cooper selects the best of the heartwood, discarding the sapwood as too porous. The staves are cut to measure, bent to shape, and shaved ever so slightly for that perfect, tight fit. They are then gathered together and bound by strong, steel hoops, with the bottom end being placed first. The barrel is then set afire inside. This charring process helps to form and release certain key chemicals in the wood. Of particular note are the vanilla-flavored compounds, so closely associated with fine Bourbon and Tennessee whiskeys, that are produced and released by the charring of the lignin and cellulose material in the wood. Also available to the new whiskey are various sugars latent in the oak, sugars with such exotic names as glucose, arabinose, fructose and xylose. Finally, the head is placed and the last of the hoops is hammered home and tightened.

After they are filled, the heads of the barrels are stencilled with pertinent information—the name of the distillery and its license, the date of filling, the quantity of whiskey in the barrel, a designation of its warehouse destination (each warehouse is most often identified by a letter of the alphabet), and a number for identifying the individual barrel. After the wooden bungs are hammered home

*Hammering
in the bung
after filling
the barrel*

Courtesy of Jack Daniel Distillery

in the bung holes of the filled barrels, the barrels (usually 50 to 53 gallons each) are loaded and hauled to the warehouses.

The design of most warehouses is what is called 'open rick.' In these, sturdy posts and beams of majestic oak lumber support row after row of barrels, often five to seven storeys high. The open rick warehouses are open to the climate. Typically sheathed with exterior walls of sheet metal, sometimes brick, with small, screened windows, they heat up during the hot summers and cool down during the cold winters.

Since the open rick warehouses are expensive to build, difficult to maintain, and provide only complicated access to the barrels (for example, if one barrel is spotted as leaking and needing repair, the only way to get to it is by rolling out the barrels in the rick with it, one by one, until you can get to the leaker), some of the larger distillers are moving towards open warehouses. With architecture recalling the inside of an airplane hangar, the vast space of these warehouses is filled by pallet after pallet of barrels stacked on end in enormous, high blocks, transported not by brute manual strength but by the forklift.

During the maturation period, much happens silently. The young whiskey interacts with the chemicals in the wood. Various tannins are leeched from the wood to the whiskey. More obviously, as the whiskey soaks into the layers of char, the charcoal absorbs certain components, acting as a charcoal filter does. Also, the sugars in the oak, caramelized and made available by the charring process, yield themselves to the whiskey, providing that distinctive vanilla-caramel sweetness associated with Bourbon and Tennessee whiskey. And as the oak breathes, certain of the more volatile, undesirable components evaporate. Thus, the fresh graininess of the white dog disappears, and the whiskey takes on color and mellows in nose and flavor. Not all that happens in the barrel is easily understandable. For example, the alcoholic strength of barrels is apt to change during the aging process. In the Scotch industry, the whisky, aged in Scotland, of course, tends to lose alcoholic strength. But in the American whiskey industry, it tends to go the other way. Especially in barrels located in the upper ricks of the open warehouses, the alcoholic proof rises year by year.

Now, *why* should this happen? There seemed to be as many answers to this question as people we asked it of. One master distiller, sucking air through his teeth when we posed the question, suggested what is known as the 'osmosis theory'—that the water molecules, being smaller than alcohol, could more easily gain passage through the oak, thus leaving the barrel at a greater rate than the alcohol. A second distiller we asked tucked his hands under his belt, gazed off into the distance for a moment, and spun a delightful story about how, as the barrels heated up in the hot summertime, the alcohol would turn to vapor within the barrel and by the increasing pressure exerted by the gases trapped within the barrel the water would be squeezed out proportionately more rapidly than the alcohol. (Maybe it was the taste testing we had already done that day, but we had a hard time following the rationale here.) Yet another hypothesis was that because it is hotter in Kentucky and Tennessee than in Scotland, the heat favored the evaporation of water over alcohol. (That one really had us stumped. Since the evaporation point of alcohol is *lower* than that of water, wouldn't you expect the *alcohol* to evaporate proportionately faster, thus lowering the proof rather than raising it?) Yet another noted distiller suggested that the year-round high humidity of Scotland favored the proportionately greater evaporation rate of alcohol there, whereas the relatively less humid climate of Kentucky (especially in the upper floors of the warehouses in the hot summer time) favors a relatively greater rate of evaporation for water. Finally, we asked this of a chemist involved in the industry, expecting to be told the authoritative scientific opinion. He paused a moment, bit his lower lip, and finally responded, "You know, I have no idea. I really can't explain it."

Whatever the reason, that's how it works.

In an interesting experiment, Maker's Mark, which sells most of its used barrels to the Glenmorangie distillery in Scotland, has been aging a barrel of Glenmorangie single-malt Scotch in one of its warehouses in Kentucky. A comparative taste test of the outcome will be both amusing and instructive.

As you walk into a warehouse, the heady, deep aroma of aging whiskey and oak lumber permeate the air. It's a warm, friendly smell that fills your nose and even seems to linger in your clothes. The workmen, rolling freshly filled barrels into their place on the ricks for aging, are clearly skilled in their tasks. The barrels must be stored with the bung on top, or else leakage is likely. Thus, as the workman guides the new barrel into the rick, he somehow has learned just where to have the bung hole as he sends the barrel rolling into the rick to rest against its mate for the next few years. If when the barrel comes to a stop, lightly touching its neighbor, its bung hole is not at the top, the workman must climb inside the rick framing, along the rails to the barrel, and man-handle it around until the bung hole does rest on top. We suppose either one learns quickly how to judge the correct positioning well ahead of time, or else one soon leaves this line of work.

The light filters in through the small screened windows, casting a golden glow, in harmony with the gold color of the aged oak timbers and barrels, as well as the increasing reddish gold color of the whiskey resting inside. As the whiskey ages, the barrels 'breathe.' In

the first year, between absorption into the new wood and evaporation, some six to eight percent of the volume will be lost. And evaporation continues, year after year, at the rate of four to five percent.
A good whiskey is likely to have lost 30 percent of its original volume by the time it is ready for bottling—clearly aging can be an
expensive proposition. How long the whiskey should be aged varies
quite a bit. Corn whiskey, as noted, tends to be aged very little. Most
Bourbons or Tennessee whiskeys spend a good four years in the
wood, though the distiller knows that individual barrels may
progress at slightly different rates. Prior to Prohibition, the average
length of aging seems to have been longer than it is now; but one
can find high quality whiskeys that have been in the wood for seven
to nine years. We had the privilege of sampling a 28-year-old Bourbon, destined for a foreign market, but found it to be rather woody
and a bit musty. Older doesn't necessarily mean better. Probably
because of the newness of the oak and the availability of the char,

*Whiskey
aging in a
traditional,
open-rick
warehouse
at Barton
Distilling*

Mark Waymack

Removing the bungs from the barrels at George Dickel

James Harris

these American whiskeys seem to mature much more rapidly than their Scottish and Irish cousins. A first-class Scotch whisky can easily improve for twelve to sixteen years in the wood, whereas a sound American whiskey might peak at somewhere between seven and nine years of age.

Finally, when the barrel is judged ready for bottling, the distiller typically collects a large number of barrels, scattered about the warehouse—some from the top ricks, some from the bottom floor, some from the periphery of the warehouse, and some from the heart of the stacks. The barrels are de-bunged and 'dumped' (emptied). Usually cut with water to a standard proof, and cold filtered to pre-vent chill haze, the whiskey is then bottled, labelled, and packed for delivery.

In a new trend, a couple of distilleries have begun to pick out exceptionally good barrels and make these available to the discriminating public. One version of this strategy is the 'single-barrel' whiskey. Here, barrels are individually selected, then dumped, filtered, cut with water to the proper strength, and bottled *one at a time.* Often, the number of the barrel and date of dumping are recorded on the label. A second strategy is the 'small batch.' Arguing that single barrels are too subject to undesirable variation, in the small-batch scheme a *limited* number of the highest-quality barrels, allowed to age much longer than usual, are chosen from the best parts of the warehouse. These are dumped together and then bottled as a 'small batch'—usually filtered and cut with water, sometimes bottled and labelled at 'barrel proof.' These special whiskeys are far more expensive than usual, reflecting not only the longer aging in the warehouse, but also the fact that there are quite limited supplies. (If you bottle all your best barrels as small batch or single-barrel, then the quality of your main label whiskey will eventually suffer.) There is no denying that the single-barrel and small-batch experiments have made available distinctive, high-quality whiskeys to which the public formerly did not have access.

Varieties and Terminology

So that the consumer knows just what he or she is getting, the distilling industry has co-operated with the federal government in coming up with some specific definitions for various whiskeys.

Blended Whiskey is made by blending a straight whiskey with a large proportion of rectified whiskey, also called neutral grain spirits. Neutral grain spirits can be made from any starchy grain, and tend to be distilled at very high proof, leaving nearly all of the complex flavoring components—the congeners—behind in the stillage. Its commercial advantages are that it is relatively inexpensive to manufacture and it has little or no taste, thus making a light tasting whiskey possible.

Bourbon must be made from a mash of not less than 51 percent corn. If the percentage of corn exceeds 80, it becomes identified as corn whiskey. The remainder is generally malted barley and rye,

Dumping whiskey at United Distillers from the barrels into a trough, from where it goes for filtering and bottling

Mark Waymack

but this is not specified, and some distillers prefer wheat to rye. Most commercial formulas seem to run around 75–78 percent corn, but many distillers are quite secretive here. Bourbon must be distilled at less than 160 proof, and aged in new, charred, oak barrels for a minimum of two years. Contrary to popular belief, Bourbon need not be made in Kentucky, though it is most closely identified with Kentucky.

Corn Whiskey must be distilled from a mash of at least 80 percent corn. Since the law does not require its aging in new, charred barrels, it tends to be aged for only a short time and in used barrels or sometimes in new, plain oak. Reflecting its Moonshine affiliation, it tends to lack the color, mellowness and smoothness of a well-aged whiskey.

Light Whiskey. In a trend that never found great favor, distillers produced a whiskey that came off the still between 160 and 189 proof. A kind of analog to 'lite' beer. This venture seems to have fallen by the wayside.

Neutral Spirits. Also called rectified whiskey, neutral spirits usually come off the still at more than 190 proof. There is almost no discernible taste or aroma other than the alcohol itself.

Rye Whiskey is whiskey made from a mash of at least 51 percent rye. A style most closely associated with Pennsylvania and Maryland. Since Prohibition, its share of the market has steadily decreased, and it is now a fairly marginal part of the American whiskey industry. As a straight whiskey, it must be aged a minimum of two years.

Straight Whiskey (which includes Bourbon, Tennessee, and Rye whiskeys) must be made of grain, it must come off the still at less than 160 proof, and it must be aged a minimum of two years in new, charred, oak barrels.

Tennessee Whiskey must be distilled from a mash of not less than 51 percent of some one grain. This means it need not be made predominantly from corn. As a matter of fact, however, Tennessee whiskey formulas closely resemble the grain proportions of Bourbons. Tennessee whiskey must be brought off the still at less than 160 proof. What makes Tennessee whiskey distinct, according to the persuasive arguing of Reagor Motlow of Jack Daniel's before the federal government's Department of the Treasury, is the unique filtering through maple charcoal, a process that takes the edge off some of the harsher compounds and emphasizes the smoothness of a full, middle body in the end product. The whiskey is filtered through as much as 18 vertical feet of maple charcoal before it is put in the barrels for aging. For this reason, Tennessee whiskey is not the same as a Bourbon whiskey.

Some of the distilleries we visited openly scorned the notion of whiskey-making as a science—rather, it is an *art;* other distilleries just as adamantly argued that good whiskey-making can only be guaranteed through good science. We, at least, have some suspicion that any such debate is ultimately unresolvable. Partly this is because one person's science may well be another person's art. Also, we have come away with the impression that the best of whiskeys are produced where there is a team spirit, a kind of symbiosis between science and art, between chemist and traditional distiller.

Perhaps the next time you take a sip of whiskey, you can come to your own judgement—science or art? Most likely, both.

3

Kentucky Bourbon

Bourbon whiskey need not necessarily be made in Kentucky, at least not by law. But there can be no doubt whatsoever that in terms of history, quality, and public awareness, Bourbon whiskey is indelibly associated with Kentucky. And virtually all Bourbons now on the market are in fact made in Kentucky.

History

The first white European exploration of this region can be dated to 1750, when a Dr. Thomas Walker was dispatched to the area by the Loyal Land Company of Virginia. But it was not until 1769 when, led by Daniel Boone, white exploration and settlement began on a significant scale. In 1774, James Harrod founded Harrodstown (now known as Harrodsburg) on the Kentucky River, which is credited with being the first 'permanent' white settlement.

Several Native American tribes competed with each other to use the area as hunting grounds, but no tribe was in permanent residence.

In 1775, Daniel Boone led a returning party, blazing a trail from the Cumberland Gap into Kentucky. By late spring he had reached the Kentucky River and established Boonesborough.

As white settlers came in ever-increasing numbers, 'Indian troubles' erupted, with the late 1770s known as particularly hard times. Legend even has it that Daniel Boone and a working party were captured in 1778 and taken north of the Ohio River towards Detroit where they were held hostage by Chief Blackfish. Boone then later escaped in time to warn Boonesborough of an impending attack, thus saving the settlement from utter destruction. The last major battle between Native Americans and white settlers came in 1782.

Chafing under a very distant rule by Virginia, Kentucky organized itself as a separate commonwealth and entered the Union in 1792 as the 15th state.

As these political trials and tribulations began to settle down, commerce also began to develop. Agriculture was, of course, the backbone of the developing economy. But getting goods delivered out of the region was not easy. A lack of affordable ground transportation made rivers the most important trade routes. The movement of goods was hampered because Spain controlled the lower Mississippi. In 1787, however, downriver trade was developing, and a trading treaty with Spain negotiated in 1795 removed most of the remaining legal barriers. The Louisiana Purchase of 1803 firmly secured downriver access.

Commercial whiskey production closely followed the development of river access. As a cottage industry, whiskey-making came along with the settlers as soon as they began farming. Able to produce crops beyond mere subsistence, but with difficulties hampering the shipment of large quantities of grain, the early settlers found that it was most profitable to convert grain into whiskey, put it into compact, spoilage-proof barrels, and then ship it down the river. The 1790s saw the first blossoming of a *commercial* whiskey industry.

Perhaps it was its relative inaccessibility that earned Kentucky whiskey its earliest designation as 'Bourbon.' Unlike whiskey produced in the regions east of the Appalachians, there was a significant time lag between the production of Kentucky whiskey and its eventual acquisition by the consumer. The distiller would store the barrels of whiskey until such time as weather made downriver shipping possible and space was available on board a river boat. The whiskey then made the slow journey down river, eventually arriving perhaps in New Orleans where it would be rerouted for further distribution—to the West or, by way of the Gulf of Mexico, to the South and East. By the time this whiskey reached a consumer's glass, the aging in the oak barrel had worked some of its magic, and the spirit was light amber colored and far more smooth and mellow than other whiskeys.

A common point of embarkation for these whiskeys for their downriver trip was Bourbon County, Kentucky, on the Ohio River. With the point of origin stencilled on the barrels, purchasers downriver began to request 'Bourbon' whiskey.

This aging process received a significant boost when, for whatever reason, the custom began of charring the inside of the barrel before filling it with new whiskey. We have discussed the origin of this practice in Chapter 1. The resulting whiskey had a deep amber color and a pronounced mellow, sweet taste.

In any event, the effects of the charring make sugars and tannins readily available to the new spirit. The whiskey aged in these barrels takes on a deep amber color and develops the characteristic sweet, caramel-vanilla flavors that are so distinctive of Bourbon.

In 1790, Kentucky's population stood at some 74,000, and whiskey was being produced. By 1990, the population had grown to 3,685,296, and whiskey remains one of Kentucky's major products.

Geography

While the human side of making whiskey in Kentucky may be full of historical accidents, from a 'natural' point of view, Kentucky's eminence as a distiller of whiskey is no surprise.

The Bourbon industry has tended to gravitate to the north-central region of Kentucky, stretching from Frankfort and Lawrenceburg in the east to Bardstown and Louisville in the west. (For some time there was a cluster of distilleries in Owensboro, far to the west of Louisville, but those facilities now all stand silent.)

This region, sometimes known as the Limestone or Bluegrass region, is also famous for its bluegrass and its thoroughbred racing

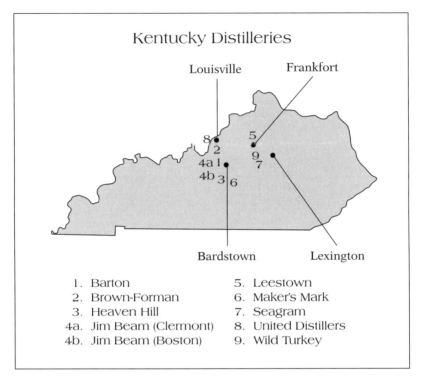

Kentucky Distilleries

1. Barton
2. Brown-Forman
3. Heaven Hill
4a. Jim Beam (Clermont)
4b. Jim Beam (Boston)

5. Leestown
6. Maker's Mark
7. Seagram
8. United Distillers
9. Wild Turkey

horses. Such a confluence is explicable. The rich limestone structure of the earth here means a high content of calcium phosphate and calcium carbonate in both the soils and the water. The phosphate is a natural fertilizer; hence plants thrive—not just bluegrass, but also corn, rye, wheat, and barley. Furthermore, the calcium-rich soil and water mean a calcium-rich diet for the animals that feed upon them. And we all know how important calcium intake is for the development of strong bones and, to a lesser extent, muscles. Hence, horses raised here might well be expected to have good growth and strength. Finally, the high calcium and phosphate content in the water make for a superb whiskey. The calcium apparently crowds out the undesirable iron contaminants; but more importantly the phosphates act as a remarkably effective nutrient boost for the yeast, encouraging an active, efficient fermentation of the mash.

The climate is also conducive to raising corn and other grains. There is ample rainfall, averaging 43 inches per year. This ensures abundant water not only for growing crops, but also for making whiskey, as well as for putting into the condenser coils to cool the spirit as it comes off the still. The growing season in this region is around 180 days. Winters are mild, and summers are warm. So the water, soil, and climate are all ideally suited for manufacturing whiskey.

The countryside here is anything but flat. Making whiskey involves moving about, including up and down, large quantities of quite heavy materials. The grain goes through the mill into the cooker, where mixed with water it cooks for several hours. It then goes to the fermenter, from there to the still, and from there to the barrel. Prior to mechanization, how was this to be accomplished? The easiest answer was to use gravity itself. It's much easier to let gravity pull the hot, heavy mash into the fermenter rather than trying to pump it up into another tank. Urban breweries would solve this problem by building breweries many storeys in height, but a six- or seven-storey building would have been pretty impractical in late eighteenth- and early nineteenth-century Kentucky. So you build your distillery as a series of small buildings cascading down a hillside. The ever-present and economically free force of gravity does the work for you.

When settlement began, forests covered some 75 percent of Kentucky. Hence, when distillers needed oak trees from which to make barrels, an abundant supply was ready at hand. Logging has cut most of those primeval forests, but aggressive efforts of the state forestry service have meant that significant forests have been recultivated. Timber and barrel-making are still important productive activities here.

Finally, the climate once again enters the picture. The warm summers (the mean temperature in July is 77 degrees Fahrenheit) and cool winters (mean temperature of 33 degrees Fahrenheit in January) seem well suited to the aging of Bourbon whiskey. In the height of summer, the upper floors of the warehouses may heat up to 120 or sometimes even 140 degrees Fahrenheit. The heat causes the whiskey to expand, forcing itself deeper into the wood of the barrel, where it mingles with the lignin, cellulose, tannins, and sugars. Then, as the cooler winter months come, the whiskey shrinks, withdrawing from the wood, so to speak, and mixing those tannins and sugars with the whiskey in the center of the barrel. Year after year, this process is repeated, deepening the amber color of the spirit, as well as accentuating its smoothness, mellowness, and its caramel-vanilla sweetness.

The Kentucky Bourbon Industry

Like any industry, Bourbon-making in Kentucky has had its share of ups and downs. From its infancy as a commercial industry in the late 1790s, the business expanded at a rapid rate, flourishing into the mid-nineteenth century. The federal government eventually learned that high taxation drove the business from legal businesses to moonshiners and that a lower tax rate actually increased overall tax revenues.

At the end of the nineteenth century the rumblings of Prohibition were heard, yet the industry was still quite active and diverse. Despite various up and down cycles in the marketplace, there were hundreds of distilleries operating in Kentucky just prior to Prohibition.

When Prohibition arrived, distilling mostly went into mothballs or into hidden clefts in the hills. Nine distilleries were given special licenses to manufacture 'medicinal whiskey,' available only by prescription. Repeal brought a host of distillers back into the business. Many of these re-opened enterprises were under-capitalized and soon folded; but many did survive.

Since Prohibition's repeal there has been a strong trend toward consolidation, a trend that rapidly accelerated in the 1980s. At present, there are only nine licensed producers of Bourbon in all of Kentucky. These are: Barton Distilling, James Beam, Brown-Forman, Heaven Hill, Leestown, Maker's Mark, Seagram, United Distillers, and Wild Turkey.

That there are only these nine may come as a surprise to most readers. After all, if you go into a well-stocked liquor store you can easily find dozens of different Bourbon labels. This situation has developed over the years because as a distillery would go out of business, or perhaps just needed ready cash, the labels it owned would be sold. For example, when United Distillers bought Medley Distilling, Fleischmann's, and National Distilling, it acquired all of the labels that these distilleries had themselves acquired over the decades. Some of these labels United Distillers would choose to keep; others would be sold off to the highest bidder. As another example, though Old Grand-Dad was for long produced at the National Distillers in Frankfort, that business was bought by American Brands, the parent company of James Beam, in the 1980s. It is now closed, and what is bottled as Old Grand-Dad is produced at the Beam plants. American Brands holds 22 labels for the domestic market. United Distillers now holds a huge inventory of brand names and labels, acquired through its acquisition of several distilling firms. Medley Distilling, for example, prior to its acquisition by United Distillers, held rights to more than 90 different labels. United Distillers is severely pruning the number of brands that it will produce. We are not sure exactly how many different labels adorn the various products of Heaven Hill, but the list is long indeed.

Another way that labels multiply is through contract distilling. In this arrangement, someone who owns a label, but has no ownership of a distillery proper, will contract with a distiller to produce the whiskey. The Van Winkle brands are an excellent example of this arrangement.

Bottles distributed in Kentucky all seem to have a special code somewhere on the label—DSP followed by a number. This represents the license number given to the producer by the State of Kentucky. Consider, thus, a bottle of "T.W. Samuels" Bourbon. Its label says it is distilled by the "Stonegate Distillery," and bottled by the "Applegate Distillery." In fine print on the back label, however is the code "KY DSP 31." "KY DSP 31" would stand for 'Kentucky Distilled Spirits Producer #31'—and in this case #31 just happens to be Heaven Hill.

But such disclosure seems not to be required everywhere. Buy a bottle of "Hancock's Reserve Single Barrel Bourbon" from a liquor store in Chicago and all that is found on the label is that it was distilled by the "Hancock Distillery, Frankfort, KY." It requires some detective work to ascertain that the Hancock Distillery is a small, one-room packaging building located on the premises of the

Leestown Distilling Company, home of Ancient Age, Ancient Ancient Age, as well as Blanton's, Rock Hill Farm, and Elmer T. Lee. Indeed, to our knowledge, there are only two Bourbon distilleries in Kentucky where all of the whiskey produced and bottled is clearly tied to the distillery's one name. They are Maker's Mark and Wild Turkey.

Now this is not as sinister as it might sound. Through the use of different formulas, different aging, and different bottling proofs, the whiskeys put into differently labelled bottles, though from the same distillery, are often quite different in character. Old Grand-Dad *is* certainly different from Jim Beam. Elijah Craig *is* indisputably different from Heaven Hill or Evan Williams. Still, there are not always such differences, and it requires special knowledge or much experience to be sure of a label's significance.

The Kentucky Distilleries

There are, then, nine active producers of Bourbon whiskey in Kentucky. The easternmost, Leestown, home of Ancient Age, is on the outskirts of Frankfort, the state capital. Wild Turkey is on the eastern edge of Lawrenceburg. And Seagram's is just to the south of Lawrenceburg. Bardstown, south of Louisville, includes Barton and Heaven Hill. The two Beam plants, Clermont and Boston, are both within a dozen miles of Bardstown. And Maker's Mark, officially at Loretto, is not far from Bardstown. Louisville is the home of two producers: Brown-Forman and United Distillers.

Visiting the Distilleries

The distilleries of Kentucky—at least the *legal* ones—are easily accessible by car and several are quite enjoyable to visit. As you plan your visit, bear in mind that most distilleries shut down for some period during the summer months: the temperature gets too hot for the best distilling, and so the hottest time is an opportunity for annual cleaning and repair work. Do call ahead to check on dates, though most distilleries keep the visitor receptions centers open even when the distillery is not distilling. Warehousing and bottling are year-round operations.

Leestown and Wild Turkey are each within a half-hour of Lexington. We recommend taking in Wild Turkey in the morning. Then have lunch at the Anderson Grill in downtown Lawrenceburg (open only for breakfast and lunch). Give the local soft drink a try, have a hot lunch (or a sandwich if your appetite is too small), and definitely save room for one of the incredible pies—banana cream pie ran a close race with coconut cream for top place the times we visited. After lunch, head up the road to the north side of Frankfort and catch Leestown Distilling, home of Ancient Age, Blanton's, Hancock's Reserve, Elmer T. Lee, and Rock Hill Farm.

As this book was in production, we learned that Brown-Forman is renovating the old Labot and Graham Distillery just outside Frankfort. Located on the site of the original Oscar Pepper Distillery, built in 1838, the building has been nominated for the National Register of Historic Landmarks and may well have already been added to the list by the time that this book appears. The Brown-Forman project is a very ambitious one indeed. The 42 acres at the site will be used to operate the refurbished distillery which will be restored to exacting standards and to operate a whiskey museum under the title of the Bourbon Heritage Homeplace. The distillery will produce a new label of small-batch Bourbon, and the museum will feature exhibits concerning the history and growth of the whiskey industry. The entire operation will be open to the public. The Bourbon Heritage Homeplace, located at the site of the Labot and Graham Distillery, will be located just two miles off US Route 60 between Versailles and Frankfort on McCracken Pike. Be sure to visit if you are in the area after the summer of 1996. If you are going to be around Lexington, you may also want to contact the Keeneland Race Course, just west of Lexington, to see when the horses are running.

The most a casual tourist can do in terms of visiting the Louisville distilleries is to drive by and take a look. Neither outfit is prepared for visitors. But Louisville is a charming city with plenty of hotel space—cheap stuff near the airport and some very nice ones downtown. We splurged and stayed at the Seelbach Hotel, and enjoyed every minute of it. The Brown also has an excellent, high-class reputation. And don't pass up a chance to visit Churchill Downs, one of the most famous horse tracks in the world, and home of the Kentucky Derby.

Bardstown has to be regarded as the center of Kentucky distilling. By car, Bardstown is 30–45 minutes south of Louisville. Jim Beam's Clermont plant, a professional at hosting tourists, is on the left, a stone's throw off the interstate as you drive south from Louisville and take the Bardstown exit. Heaven Hill, in Bardstown itself, offers a pleasant, informative tour. Maker's Mark, with an excellent visitor reception center and delightful tour, is in Loretto, a short, though winding, drive south of Bardstown.

Not to be missed in Bardstown is the Oscar Getz Museum of Whiskey History. Founded through an endowment from Oscar Getz and his family (the founder of Barton Distilling), this museum has an unparalleled collection of early whiskey bottles and jugs, some small pot stills, and early manuscripts and books pertaining to whiskey. The museum is a treasure trove for the historian, the idle tourist, or the whiskey aficionado. The museum is housed in Spalding Hall, at 114 North Fifth Street. The telephone number is (502) 348-2999.

Each fall, around the third weekend of September, Bardstown has been sponsoring a 'Bourbon Festival,' with educational displays, blind tastings, and other paraphernalia. For more information, give the Bardstown Information Center (or the Oscar Getz Museum) a call.

We always stay at The Park View Inn, operated by 'Toogie,' when we visit Bardstown. (It's quite possible to stay in Louisville and just drive down for the day; but that takes some of the charm out of your visit.) Kurtz's restaurant, attached to the Park View Inn, is quite reliable. There are also a couple of restaurants on Third Avenue, the main street through town.

And don't leave town without stopping at Toddy's Liquor, established by Toddy Beam. One obvious reason for doing this is to check out the Bourbon stock; but another reason is to buy a box of Bourbon Fudge made by the monks of Gethsemani. This marriage of chocolate and Kentucky Bourbon is, indeed, heavenly. Follow the directions on the box and keep it refrigerated once you get home (if it lasts that long). And think twice about giving any to the kids.

Unlike the geographic *appellations* of the French wine industry, it cannot be said that different geographic locations in Kentucky lead to discernible taste differences. There is no 'Bardstown style' distinct from a 'Frankfort style' or 'Louisville style.' For the purposes of organizing the individual accounts of the different Bourbons produced here, we will simply use some semblance of alphabetical ordering.

Barton Distilling Company

Barton Distilling is not flashy. It is not gimmicky. It is not famous. Jerry Dalton, the chief chemist, says, "We're a low profile company. A lot of people don't even know that Barton exists, even though we are the eighth largest producer of spirits in the country." Barton eschews the cult of personality. The Barton philosophy is not to focus on the person who makes the whiskey; rather, it is to focus on the *whiskey*.

Judging from our experience with Barton's Bourbons, this philosophy serves Barton well. The distillery and its product deserve more recognition than they have received.

As Barton Distilling, the company dates to around 1944, when a firm of that name, created by the Oscar Getz family in the post-Prohibition 1930s, acquired the present distillery. Distilling at this site, just more than a mile from the heart of Bardstown, goes back to at least the 1880s. We know that in 1876, Tom Moore and Ben Mattingly bought a distillery in this vicinity, changing its name to the Mattingly and Moore Distillery. Then, apparently having sold the Mattingly and Moore Distillery to John Simms and R.H. Edelen, Moore, along with Mattingly, opened the Tom Moore Distillery in 1889, just a stone's throw away from the present site of Barton's.

In the *Nelson County Record* of 1896, the Tom Moore Distillery is described as having a capacity of 200 bushels a day, using a formula of 60 percent corn and 40 percent small grains. No "branch water" is used—the distillery being supplied entirely from limestone rich springs. In an accolade that could be applied to the current management, it states that Moore "tries to obtain quality more than quantity."

Prohibition closed the Tom Moore Distillery as well as the Mattingly and Moore facility. But in 1934, following Repeal, the Tom Moore Distillery was acquired and modernized by Harry Teur. Much of the machinery was replaced; and many of the old wood-frame buildings were rebuilt in brick and concrete.

The Barton distillery in the 1950s

The Oscar Getz family, having been in the whiskey industry since shortly after the repeal of Prohibition, but not owning a Bourbon production facility, purchased the distillery in 1944. At first they retained the Tom Moore name, but eventually changed the plant's name to the Barton Distilling Company. It is unclear where the name 'Barton' came from. According to one account it hearkens back to a Barton Distillery, long since defunct, in Cynthiana, Kentucky. Another, equally plausible story is that the Getz family put a bunch of names in a hat, and 'Barton' was picked out.

As well as supplying the world with a high-quality Bourbon, Oscar Getz also endowed the Oscar Getz Museum of Whiskey History, in downtown Bardstown, a Mecca for anyone interested in whiskey and its place in American history.

The distiller at Barton is Bill Friel, but Jerry Dalton, as chemist, and Friel obviously work closely together as a team. Dalton's philosophy is simple yet complex. A technical term for his management approach is 'statistical process control,' or 'S.P.C.,' as he refers to it. A more colorful way of putting the idea is, 'Mundane events, mystical processes.'

Dalton's strategy is to so tightly control the whiskey-making process that luck plays no part. So, as he explained, "When I became

Jerry Dalton, chief chemist at Barton, checking the mash

responsible for the distillery, I decided you had to have some targets, with allowable parameters." But Dalton at first had no data-
base from which to derive his targets. "So I analyzed the historical
data, lab sheets, going back eight to ten years. From that I identified the averages and the scatter. By analyzing the historical data, I
know how the distillery operated before I came. This way we can
guarantee quality, consistency, and continuity. We have a firm hand
on the Barton process. As people retire, we can still produce the
same quality product."

It is this process-control frame of mind that leads Dalton to his own hypothesis of why the practice of charring the barrels began: Economically pinched distillers used wooden barrels for many purposes, one being the fermenting tub. Now, such distillers would not have known anything about bacteria or germ theories, but they could easily have figured out that scorching a barrel after one fermentation and before the next would help assure a better fermentation. Then, because you could only burn the inside so much before threatening the barrel itself, they would convert it from a fermenting tub into an aging barrel where the whiskey would end up interacting with the layer of char.

The idea is that whiskey is made by a *process;* it just so happens that individual persons take various roles in facilitating this process. And once the process is understood, and to the extent that it is understood, it is not particularly material just *who* shepherds the process. What *is* important is that the process be kept within its proper boundaries. And this happens when each individual knows his or her job and performs it.

Thus, when people ask Jerry Dalton what he 'does' for a living, instead of giving some fancy title, he likes simply to say, 'I make whiskey,' with the emphasis falling upon *whiskey,* for that's the point.

Indeed, it does work. Barton Distilling now has about 15 workmen earning wages and five salaried staff workers. Although actively distilling only about half of each year, during that period they mash 5,800 bushels a day, thus filling 17 fermenters and producing about 153,000 proof gallons each week. That translates into around 2,300 barrels a week.

The distillery still sits where the Tom Moore Distillery did, in a deep ravine, with the warehouses on the hills, hundreds of feet up, behind the distillery.

The water still comes from various limestone springs, including the old Tom Moore spring. Some is collected in a lake, now called Teur's Lake, presumably named for Harry Teur, the man who reopened the facility after Prohibition.

Statistical Process Control begins with inspecting and analyzing the grain as it comes in. Does it meet standards of cleanliness? What is its moisture content? Does it meet specifications for quality?

Rolling newly filled whiskey barrels to the warehouse

Mark Waymack

The cooking is monitored, to know that the starches are being appropriately rendered. The activity of the fermenters is carefully recorded. What are their temperatures? What should the temperature be? When the temperature fluctuates outside of normal parameters, what does the distilled spirit taste like? Is the fermentations proceeding at the appropriate rate? An attemperator is used to maintain the fermenters at an ideal temperature for the yeasts to do their task.

The still is primarily a stainless steel construction, but between a copper upper section and loads of scrap copper loaded onto the sieve trays inside the upper part of the column, everything works to order.

The low wines come off the beer still at 125 proof and then enter the copper doubler. Once again, the activity is carefully monitored and controlled. What is the temperature at the top of the column of the still? Fluctuations too far from the norm may result in too many fusel oils or aldehydes, or perhaps too much water. Past records and long experience tell the distiller whether he is using too much or too little steam. The white dog comes out of the doubler at 135 proof. It is then cut with pure water and put in the barrel at 125 proof.

Barton maintains 30 active warehouses. Each is seven storeys tall; each is naturally ventilated; and each is capable of holding some 25,000 barrels of aging spirit.

During the aging process, a sample of each and every entry is tested, looking in fairly objective terms for that special Barton blend of organoleptic qualities. And testing continues at regular intervals.

What is that special Barton blend of 'organoleptic properties'? Bill Friel and Jerry Dalton both agree that Barton Bourbon is special. As Dalton puts it in a typical example of Southern understatement, "Everybody's going to tell you, 'Boy, our whiskey's smooth, real smooth.' But I've drunk a lot of whiskey, and Barton does right well."

Barton Bourbon has the desirable barrel tones of a good Bourbon, but it is noticeably less sweet than many, intentionally so, we are told. It is full-bodied, with a comparably full flavor, and a touch of what might be called the 'Barton bite,' just enough to remind you that this is not some 100-year-old French cognac, but good American Bourbon. Finally, there is a nice, smooth, lingering finish—once again, not too sweet.

Bill Friel and Jerry Dalton deliver what they promise—a high-quality, individualistic, complex Bourbon. And perhaps far more than any other distillery, they are working at a promise that the same, high-quality Barton Bourbon will still be made and available, long after they have ceased to be around.

Remember, it's the *whiskey* that's important!

TASTING NOTES

Very Old Barton, 40 percent
Judging from its color, we would guess that this is around eight years old. Perhaps it is a mixture of different ages. There is an initial floral-woody combination in the aroma. The full-bodied whiskey is dry for a Bourbon, probably reflecting a

relatively high proportion of small grains. The sugars tend toward the malty-wood side, rather than more typical Bourbon vanilla-caramel tones. There is a signature 'Barton bite'—certainly not a harshness, but rather an assertive firmness.

Barton now also bottles straight Bourbon under the labels Kentucky Gentleman and Kentucky Tavern.

VISITING

Barton Distilling is not really equipped for the casual visitor.

Brown-Forman

Since its inception in 1870, the Brown-Forman Corporation's philosophy of distilling has been clear and consistent: Deliver a product that the consumer can trust. This works out in at least three ways. First, maintain quality and consistency. Second, prevent adulteration. And third, be true to your label.

Over the intervening years, the Brown-Forman Corporation, by sticking to this philosophy, has grown into a major producer of spirits in America. Yet it's less well-known by its corporate name than by the names of its products. Brown-Forman now holds some wine interests, Canadian Mist, and Southern Comfort. But its roots have always been in straight whiskey, and in that line they hold three major brands: Old Forester, Early Times, and Jack Daniel's. Since Jack Daniel's is a Tennessee whiskey, the reader can find more information on it in the next chapter. Here we will focus upon the Brown-Forman straight whiskeys produced at the Louisville distillery. The first is a Bourbon, Old Forester, and the second is what Brown-Forman now markets domestically as a "Kentucky whiskey"—Early Times.

The Brown family, emigrants from Scotland to Virginia, were among the first Europeans to settle in Kentucky. William Brown, the patriarch, had been a scout for Daniel Boone before settling in Kentucky. Two generations later, George Garvin Brown founded the distillery in Louisville in 1870.

In 1870, the packaging of retail goods was quite different than it is today. From cloth to foodstuffs, domestic goods were seldom, if ever, pre-packaged. Typically, shoppers were expected to provide their own cloth bags, wooden boxes, crates, or whatever, to carry their purchases home.

Whiskey was no exception. Whiskey left the distillery in its barrel. It went through the wholesaler, and arrived at the retail establishment still in its barrel. A tap would be inserted, and whiskey

*Headquarters of
Brown-Forman*

Mark Waymack

drawn off to fill glasses or jugs at the consumer's request. There
were jugs and occasional bottles that were produced with a certain
whiskey's name on them; but they were still filled at the retail establishment, not at the distillery.

Barkeeps, unfortunately, share some of the moral failings of the
rest of the population, and adulteration of whiskey is not unheard
of. Even today, agents of the federal Alcohol, Tobacco and Firearms
agency frequent bars, armed with their distilled spirits hydrometers,
to measure the alcoholic strength of the contents of the bottles.
And occasionally, a barkeep is caught having added water to his
whiskeys.

Well, it was no different in the nineteenth century. Wooden barrels offered an easy package to tamper with. Water could be added; even the name could be changed. And so consumers had little in the way of a guarantee that what they received was what it was really supposed to be.

George G. Brown's idea, then, was to package his whiskey in a way that would minimize the chances of adulteration. His solution was to take advantage of the recently revolutionized glass-making industry. He would buy glass bottles—bottles that had only recently become economically affordable for only one-time use—and fill them with his whiskey *at his distillery*, thus guaranteeing the quality and reliability of the product. The wording that Brown wanted for his first label is used to this day on bottles of Old Forester: "This whisky is distilled by us only, and we are responsible for its richness and fine quality. Its elegant flavor is solely due to original fineness developed with care. *There is nothing better in the market.* George Garvin Brown." Thus, Brown became the first distiller to customarily bottle his whiskey at the distillery.

An early bottle of Old Forester

Courtesy of Brown-Forman

Just where George G. Brown got the idea for the name of his whiskey is a matter of great speculation. Several theories compete with each other. Initially, the whiskey was called 'Old Forrester,' with two r's. For that reason, some folks have inferred that he named it after a well-known officer in the Confederate Army—General Nathan Bedford Forrest. A second theory contends that the name was chosen to have market appeal to all the men working in the timber industry in that region. A third theory is that it was named after an insurance plan known as the 'Order of Foresters.' And a fourth is that it was named with Brown's personal physician in mind—Dr. Forrester.

Early in the business, Brown accepted a relative from Ireland, James Thompson, as a partner in the business. But in 1890, Thompson started Glenmore Distilling, which is now in the hands of United Distillers. In the meantime, George Forman, apparently the accountant, became a partner. But his portion of the business was bought up by Brown upon Forman's death. Nevertheless, the name—Brown-Forman—stuck.

When Prohibition went into effect, Brown-Forman, under the leadership of Brown's son, Owsley, applied for and was granted one of the ten licenses for the production of 'medicinal whiskey.' Prior to Prohibition, Old Forester had been what we would today call a blended whiskey. That is, a certain portion of straight whiskey would be blended with a portion of neutral spirits. But with the government regulations concerning medicinal whiskey, Brown-Forman shifted to bottling Old Forester as a straight, unblended whiskey, at 100 proof. And it remains that to this day, with the sole exception that an 86 proof version is also now bottled.

Old Forester Kentucky Straight Bourbon Whisky (Brown-Forman prefers the Scottish spelling) starts with high quality grain— an educated guess would be about 80 percent corn, with the rest split between rye and malt.

After a hot cook, the mash heads to the carbon steel fermenters. The backset is mixed in, and a strong, pure yeast is pitched. There are twelve fermenters, each having a capacity of around 40,000 gallons. Under peak operating conditions, Brown-Forman is mashing enough each day for three fermenters. The fermentation then runs typically for four days, though sometimes it can be left as long as seven, an unusually long ferment given that the industry norm seems to run three to four days.

Checking progress of the cook

Mark Waymack

When the fermentation is complete, and the Old Forester process does appear to allow time for a more complete fermentation of the sugars in the mash, the distillers beer is pumped into the beer well, and then to the beer still.

The still, made by Vendome, has a stainless steel bottom and a copper head. As the spirit comes off the still, it is at about 118 proof—fairly low compared to other distilleries. But from the beer still, it goes into the thumper for a more serious second distillation than is common. As the spirit comes off the thumper and through the tail boxes, it is at 140 proof. Because of the cook, the yeast strain, and the long fermentation, Brown-Forman is able to get about 5.3 proof gallons per bushel of grain—perhaps the highest yield in the industry.

In the cistern, it is cut with water to 125 proof and then pumped into the barrels. At this point, a significant difference emerges between Old Forester and Early Times. By law, Bourbon must go into new, charred, oak barrels. And that is what happens to Old Forester. Since these are virgin barrels, the layer of char has much to offer the new spirit—the sugar and caramel flavorings that are so distinctive of Bourbon.

Early Times (at least the domestic version) does *not* go into new barrels. Seeking to offer a lighter, less woody spirit, Brown-Forman puts Early Times into used barrels. So, while the whiskey qualifies as a straight whiskey, it is not a Bourbon. Not only does this produce a lighter tasting whiskey—less sweet, less caramel, less woody char—it also means a less expensive product, since the barrels need not be purchased new. Early Times, therefore, is not a Bourbon; nor is it a blended whiskey. Brown-Forman has managed, therefore, to have Early Times recognized by the government as a "Straight Kentucky Whiskey."

Demand is running high. Consequently, the Louisville distillery is operating seven days a week, and for most of the year. If you pushed the plant, it could mash 6,000 bushels per day. When we visited, the operation was running at around 4,500 bushels per day. It shuts down for about three to four weeks in the summer, when the weather is hottest, because it becomes impossible to run the drying operation for the spent grains. They use this opportunity to clean up the plant and to do special maintenance.

To get Old Forester, a melding of ages is used. While four years is the minimum age of any whiskey in Old Forester, each bottle is likely to contain a mixture of four-, five-, six-, and even eight-year-old whiskeys. The various chosen barrels are dumped into a holding tank, where the flavors are allowed to 'meld' or 'marry' before bottling.

We are eagerly anticipating the new small-batch Bourbon which Brown-Forman will produce at the Labot and Graham Distillery, currently being renovated. The introduction of a brand new label and bringing on line a new operation at a new site is big news in the whiskey industry! Plans call for the refurbished distillery to be up and running by the summer of 1996. Of course, the whiskey produced there will have to be aged; so there will be a wait of several years before any of us can sample this new small-batch Bourbon. The intention of the company, according to Lois Mateus of Brown-Forman, is to produce "the best Bourbon made anywhere." Our best guess is that it won't appear for at least six or eight more years—

maybe just in time for us to include tasting notes in our second (or third) edition!

TASTING NOTES

Old Forester comes in 100 proof and 86 proof.

Old Forester, 50 percent

This is a very distinctive, perhaps idiosyncratic, Bourbon. It has a pronounced, big, signature, floral bouquet. We suspect this might be the result of a pronounced presence of certain alcohols, such as ethyl acetate, that are present in other Bourbons at much lower levels. This probably bears some relation to Old Forester's long fermentation as well as its distilling proofs. For whatever reasons, though, the bouquet is *big*. This floweriness carries through on the palate, where the whiskey is intense, yet anything but heavy. Caramel and vanilla are detectable, but quite subdued, very much in the background. Finally, there is a certain 'Zing' in its finish. This is not your 'classic,' heavy, caramel-sweet Bourbon. But Old Forester fans are devoted to it; and if you ever try to slip them something different, they will most certainly let you know!

Early Times, 40 percent

The aroma is slightly less pronounced than Old Forester. On the palate, the use of used cooperage is evident in that the whiskey is quite light. There are only the subtlest of barrel tones. On the other hand, this is clearly not some unaged corn liquor. Any graininess and the more unpleasant, volatile congeners have yielded to the aging process.

VISITING

Brown-Forman corporate offices are on the west side of Louisville, with the distillery itself a couple of miles south of their offices off Dixie Highway. They are not really set up for tourists.

Heaven Hill Distillers, Inc.

Heaven Hill is, to our knowledge, the only remaining family-owned Bourbon distiller. The story begins more than 60 years ago with the five Shapira brothers—Gary, Mose, George, Edward, and David. Inheriting a small dry goods store in New Haven, Kentucky, through industry and entrepreneurial skill, they parleyed it into a small chain of stores. With sufficient capital behind them, they entered the real estate business. Then shortly after the repeal of Prohibition, they entered the distilling business in 1935.

The land they bought for the distillery had originally been staked out as a farm by a William Heavenhill, around the end of the eighteenth century. And through a clerical error somewhere along the way, which they decided not to undo, the distillery became known as Heaven Hill.

Seeking to expand in the post-World War II era, the Shapira brothers were working with a Louisville bank, trying to get a sizable loan, when the banker had the auspicious idea of pairing them up with Harry Homel, a Chicago financier. Homel had been tutored in the whiskey business in a partnership with Oliver Jacobson and Harry Blum. The successful whiskey brokering partnership had shifted when Harry Blum decided to buy out Jim Beam's share of James B. Beam Distilling. Homel was impressed with the business savvy, as well as the quality of the whiskey produced by the master distiller, Earl Beam, great-great grandson of the legendary Jacob Beam.

Early in its history, Heaven Hill pursued what is known as the 'bulk' concept—essentially a futures market. The broker or wholesaler purchases the whisky as soon as it enters the barrel. They then pay Heaven Hill warehousing costs while the barrels lie racked in the Heaven Hill warehouses. When the owner wishes to take possession of the whiskey, all he must do is pay the government tax. In this way, risk is mostly shifted by Heaven Hill to the purchaser: if

Craig Beam at the fermenters at Heaven Hill

James Harris

the demand for Bourbon slacks off, then the whiskey is of less value than the purchaser had expected, whereas if demand is much higher, then the owner can make unexpected profits. The Shapira brothers' idea was that while this means that Heaven Hill might lose out on some windfall profits, it makes for more predictable, less risky finances.

Although Heaven Hill bottles a great deal of whiskey under its own name (its Evan Williams is the third largest selling label in the country), it still produces a significant quantity of bulk whiskey for other distilleries and other brokers. Though it is hard to know for sure, we suspect that Heaven Hill whiskey is sold under more different labels than any other distillery's.

Located on the fringe of Bardstown (and part of the Bardstown Tourmobile tours) Heaven Hill is still owned and operated by the Shapiras and the Homels. Capacity has grown over the years, through several expansions, and now stands at 400 barrels per day. Earl Beam, the first Master Distiller, has been succeeded by his son, Parker Beam. And Craig Beam is destined to one day succeed his father, Parker, in that role.

When asked what makes Heaven Hill Bourbons special, Craig Beam answers succinctly and with no hesitation, "It's the care with which we watch over it. We do it the old fashioned way, using a recipe handed down in my family for generations—a recipe that we *know* works well. So, we're not going to be changing anything."

The water comes from reliable limestone springs on the distillery property. From the springs, it is pooled in several holding ponds, where it is available for the mash as well as for the cooling.

Since it is the whole process that makes Heaven Hill what it is, Craig Beam and Michael Sonne, of quality control, are not shy about revealing the basic formula. The Heaven Hill Bourbon products are made from 78 percent corn, a low 10 percent rye, and 12 percent malted barley. Craig says the rye content is kept low in order to make a less coarse, more refined spirit. For the contract distilling, the formula may well be different. This is especially true for the corn whiskey that is produced here and marketed under several labels, including the 'Georgia Moonshine' label.

The mash cooking is done in traditional, non-pressurized cookers. The sour mash 'set back' is unusually high by industry standards—about 30 percent.

The two fermenting rooms give one a sense of the large size and high activity of Heaven Hill. One room contains 17 fermenters, averaging around 15,000 gallons each. The second room has 13 fermenters, each with a capacity of 50,000 gallons. Presumably second only to James B. Beam Distilling in holdings, Heaven Hill warehouses have a capacity of more than 500,000 barrels.

The yeast, so Beam tells us, has been in his family for some 200 years. As the white dog comes off the still and collects in the cistern, Michael Sonne explains, three individuals, from distilling and from quality control, taste the spirit, checking for the appropriate Heaven Hill properties. Then it's off to the barrels for aging.

Unlike many distilleries that use the deepest char, a #4, Heaven Hill makes use of a #3 char. Sonne's argument, affirmed with a nod from Craig Beam, is that a #4 char would be something of an overkill, that Heaven Hill is looking for a balance of components in its Bourbon products, and that the #3 char just works better for them.

Michael Sonne checking the barrel dumping at Heaven Hill

Mark Waymack

When the whiskey is dumped from the barrels, it is again taste-tested by at least three key individuals. If there are ever any problems, controlled blind testing is done by 15 trained tasters before proceeding any further. The whiskey is then chilled to 25 degrees Fahrenheit, and charcoal filtered. Afterwards, it is taste-tested again.

To further our education, Sonne had lined up a representative tasting for us in the quality control laboratory.

By seven years of age, the spirit has certainly lost any graininess, so evident in the new spirit, the white dog. It is a full-bodied Bourbon, with rich amber coloring. It is smooth on the palate, without being soft. The twelve-year-old is noticeably darker. (10 percent darker by standardized testing—the most rapid change in coloring takes place in the first three years.) The twelve-year-old is also more complex and somewhat smoother. Mellow would be a good adjective. We also had the rare chance to try a 28-year-old Bourbon, destined for a foreign market. This has become an altogether different drink. The extra years have made it much heavier than the younger versions. The wood is quite noticeable, and the balance is altered. It seems more like an old brandy than a Bourbon. While the 28-year-old is not our preference, the Heaven Hill folks assure us that it has a devoted market abroad, mostly in Japan.

Finally, it is bottled.

Heaven Hill sells a great deal of whiskey to other distillers and brokers, and it often takes the skills of a Sherlock Holmes to deduce a particular bottle's origins at Heaven Hill. But the distillery seems to focus most upon its Heaven Hill label, the Evan Williams label, and its relatively new, super-premium label, Elijah Craig.

Heaven Hill is widely available as a six-year-old at 90 proof. The Evan Williams label, named after one of Kentucky's earliest distillers, comes typically at seven years of age and at 90 proof.

Max Shapira (the current Executive Vice President), Michael Sonne and Craig Beam, however, are all eager and enthusiastic in their accounts of the Elijah Craig label. Named after the legendary (a few benighted heathen say mythical) Elijah Craig, the minister-distiller credited in Bourbon-lore with the introduction of charred barrels, is left in the wood for twelve years and then bottled at a solid 94 proof. As Shapira explains, "We feel that consumers of Bourbon, especially the finer whiskeys, attribute great significance to age and proof factors. The market is telling us this, but some of us [in the industry] aren't listening. While consumers may be drinking less, in many cases they are drinking more selectively." Elijah Craig is meant to fill that super premium niche.

TASTING NOTES

Evan Williams, seven-year, 45 percent
An aromatic yet firm nose. The taste is exactly what one expects from a Bourbon: medium-bodied, smooth, with touches of vanilla-sweetness. A fine, archetypal Bourbon.

Evan Williams Single Barrel, 43.3 percent
These bottles emphasize their 'vintage' status. Thus ours noted its date of distillation as August of 1986. But the bottle doesn't tell you when it was dumped and bottled. We would guess around eight years, for our sample. There are strong similarities to the Evan Williams seven year. There is an aromatic bouquet, with malty tones. On the palate, the whiskey is medium-bodied, probably reflecting its high corn content, rounded, and mild. There are touches of caramel and sweetness. Barrel tones are subdued.

Elijah Craig, 12 year, 47 percent

A warm, amber color. The aroma is smooth, and a little more malty than vanilla. This is definitely full bodied on the palate. The flavor is typical of a classic Bourbon. A high corn content is evident, as are vanilla and lighter caramel tones from the barrel. This twelve-year version is not as flowery as its younger siblings, but mellow would be a very appropriate adjective.

Henry McKenna Single Barrel, 50 percent, 10 years old

This bears a strong similarity to the Evan Williams Single Barrel, 1987. The high percentage of corn in the mash is evident in the nose and on the palate. The higher proof and extra two years do, however, make for a slightly heavier and more intense drink which still retains its Heaven Hill edge.

Elijah Craig 18 year old Single Barrel

This whiskey is a bit more mellow, both in nose and mouth, than the other Heaven Hill Bourbons. Despite 18 years in the barrel, however, it retains a fairly light body and just a bit of an edge. While there is not the depth that more small grains could offer, there is a strength in the flowery esters, and the extra years contribute more caramel and vanilla tones and more roundness than other Heaven Hill Bourbons. It is, surprisingly, not at all 'woody'.

VISITING

Heaven Hill is easily accessible from Bardstown and welcomes visitors. From the beginning of June until Labor day, a free Tourmobile runs four times daily, departing from the downtown Bardstown Tourist Information Center. This includes a tour of the Heaven Hill Distillery. Alternatively, drop by on your own. The distillery is located off Highway 49 (Loretto Road), at the south edge of Bardstown. You might want to call ahead: 502-585-1180.

James B. Beam
Distilling Company

The Beam name is inextricably bound to Bourbon. And while James B. Beam Distilling Company might not be owned by Beam hands, the distilling itself is managed by Beam descendants, traceable in an unbroken line of commercial distillers back to 1795.

Jim Beam Bourbons outsell every other Bourbon distiller in both the national and international markets. And so we were expecting a large operation when we visited, and that is certainly what we found. We began with a tour, available to the public, of the Jim Beam plant at Clermont. But our real introduction to Jim Beam Bourbons came over lunch with F. Booker Noe, Jr., Jim Beam's grandson, currently Master Distiller Emeritus, and (judging from what everyone at other distilleries told us) the recognized Dean of Bourbon.

The story begins with Jacob Beam, packing the family goods (including a copper pot still), and with his family crossing the Appalachian Mountains through the Cumberland Gap in 1788. Settling in the area, Jacob Beam began farming and using his still to convert his corn, rye and barley into whiskey. Then, with his son David helping, his distilling operation went commercial in 1795 with the sale of the first barrel of Beam whiskey.

With the death of Jacob, in 1818, David Beam took the reins. His son, David M. Beam, was born in 1833, and joined the family business as a young man. David M.'s son, James Beauregard Beam (the 'Jim Beam') was born in 1864, and entered the family business in 1880. In 1890, D.M. Beam and Son were making just over nine barrels a day (the two Beam plants of today can together produce over 1,300 barrels a day). And in 1892, David M. Beam, citing old age, turned the business over to his son, Jim Beam, and his son-in-law, Albert J. Hart.

The *Nelson County Record* wrote in 1896 that Jim Beam and Albert Hart "are known as being among the best practical distillers

Mark Waymack

The main building of James B. Beam Distilling at Clermont

in the county." The *Record* also states that "the product is not to be excelled by anyone." The plant was capable of mashing 150 bushels of grain per day, and had three warehouses, holding altogether over 10,000 barrels. (The 55 Beam warehouses of today can hold a total of more than one million barrels.) It is also said of Jim Beam that he "enjoys the comfort of life at his country residence, where he entertains with lavish hands." The one and only product of the Beam and Hart Distillery was 'Old Tub' straight Bourbon whiskey.

Prohibition closed the distillery, and it was Jim Beam who had the sad duty of shutting down the operation. As Booker tells it, "Jim Beam, my grandfather, was 55 years old when Prohibition hit. He was 70 years old when the law was repealed. But I can show you his letter applying in 1933 for a license to distill. He must have had a lot of motivation to come back at that age. Being 70 years old, Jim

Beam did get up and go down there and built this distillery. And of course, it's not just the still. You have to set up the boiler room to generate the steam to cook with. You have to set up your warehouses to age the liquor. You have to get it all together. But, by damn, he gets it going." One problem with starting a distillery from scratch, so to speak, is that it is a good four years between the time you start your investment and when you sell your first barrels of Bourbon. As Booker explains, "Bourbon really needs to be in the barrel at least four years before it's really worth drinking. So it takes quite a bit of money to build up your stock. You have to be buying grain, coal to fire for heat to cook and distill, and barrels to put the whiskey in. You also have employees to pay. And for at least four years you get nothing back."

Now many of the ventures that started right after Prohibition suffered from undercapitalization. And with the economy still suffering from the Great Depression, making a go of the business was difficult. So Jim Beam joined up with Harry Blum of Chicago, who had proven successful in the marketing end of the business. Thus, while many of the upstart distilleries disappeared in the first few years after Prohibition, the Beam operation, producing 'Old Tub' Bourbon, pulled through. Finally, in 1942, the 'Jim Beam' label was added.

In 1945, Blum bought out Jim Beam's share of the business. And Jim Beam died in 1947, at the age of 83. His son, Jeremiah Beam carried on the family tradition, working at the distillery until he died in 1977, aged 77.

In 1967, the operation was acquired by American Brands. But the Beam family remains deeply involved at the distillery. T. Jeremiah Beam long worked at the plant, as did Jim Beam's nephew, Carl Beam, who served as master distiller for many years. Baker Beam (Carl's son), the sixth generation of Beams in distilling, was for some time the Jim Beam Master Distiller), while his brother, David Beam is a supervisor (there is currently no Master Distiller). And Freddie B. Noe II, Jim Beam's great-grandson, also works at the distillery. (The Beam family's involvement in distilling also extends beyond the Jim Beam distillery. John H. Beam, a grandson of the legendary Jacob Beam, was Vice President of Early Times in 1896, and his son, Edward D. Beam was the General Manager. More recently, Parker Beam, a sixth generation Beam, is the Master Distiller at Heaven Hill, where his son, Craig Beam, is the equivalent of Master-Distiller-To-Be.) The public persona for Jim Beam Bourbon, however, is clearly and unmistakably F. Booker Noe, Jr., Jim Beam's grandson.

Born in 1929, Booker Noe, Jr., entered the distilling business in 1951, after attending college, and although technically he is now the Master Distiller Emeritus, Booker keeps up with the day-to-day workings at Beam's two plants, Clermont and Boston, Kentucky. His reputation among the Bourbon community is remarkable. Nearly everywhere we visited we were asked, 'Have you seen Booker yet?' And if the answer was 'Not yet,' then the follow-up was, 'Well, Booker can explain this.' Or, 'Well, Booker would know that.' Or, 'Booker can tell you all about that.' Or, 'If you're really lucky, Booker'll let you have a taste of his cider from the barrel—that's something you'll never forget.'

Booker is a force to reckon with, a huge man with a storehouse of energy and a love of life. Whether it's fishing in Alaska or in the more humble distillery ponds, smoking a ham in his own smokehouse, or cooking a whole pig for a party, Booker exhibits a shining talent and an irrepressible zest for life. And that includes an extraordinary talent for making fine Bourbon and a zest for drinking the fruits of his labor. One of two grandsons of Jim Beam, Booker has for long lived in the stately brick home that was Jim Beam's own house. A home where he acquired not only Jim Beam's shotgun, but also his taste and skill in matters of whiskey.

Well, we did meet Booker. He did tell us more than we could possibly remember—about Jim Beam, about Bourbon, about fishing. We did get lucky, and had a taste of his cider from the barrel. And we even had the pleasure of a home-cooked meal, compliments of his patient, talented, and charming wife, Annis, followed by enough Bourbon lore to fill several books, and enough Bourbon to illustrate each footnote.

Under Booker's tenure, the Beam distilleries have grown in size and reputation. Faced with under-capacity at the Clermont plant, a second plant was opened just a few miles away in Boston, Ken-

*F. Booker
Noe, Master
Distiller
Emeritus of
Jim Beam*

Mark Waymack

tucky in 1953. Although there are 22 labels in the American Brands whiskey family, there are basically only two Bourbon formulas. Nevertheless, variations in the process—proportions of grains, strain of yeast, proof of distillation, and aging—result in several distinctively different styles.

It all starts, of course, with the water. And like all classic Bourbon distilleries, Jim Beam uses only sweet, limestone water.

The second ingredient is the grain. Booker insists that only high grade grains be used. The corn comes mostly from Indiana, though some is from Kentucky. But it must be of high quality to begin with, and then properly stored to prevent any mustiness. A little of it is white corn, but about 99 percent is #2 yellow corn. The rye and the

barley come from a bit farther north, where the colder, shorter growing season favors them. The classic Beam formula uses a high percentage of corn, and a relatively large percentage of rye, with the
remainder being malted barley. The second formula, the Old Grand-
Dad family of Bourbons, producing a heavier-bodied and drier-tast-
ing whiskey, lowers the percentage of corn, while substantially increasing the rye.

The large grains are cooked gently and slowly, breaking down
cell walls and rendering the starches more accessible to the enzymes
of the malt. No pressure-cooking is allowed at Jim Beam. Next is
the yeast. Yeast is important not only for what is produces—
alcohols—but also for what it leaves behind. Different strains of
yeast will each yield a different finished distiller's beer. And some of
those differences will carry through the distilling process into the
finished spirit. The yeast that Booker uses is the one isolated by his
grandfather, Jim Beam, and kept as a 'sweet yeast.' A malt-rich mash
is boiled with some hops to create a sterile, maltose-rich culture
medium.

As Booker tells it, "1933 is when he got a spontaneous-type yeast,
off of some grain. My grandmother said that he stunk up the whole
house with that yeast before he got ready to start down there right
after Prohibition. The whole house smelled like fermenting mash.
He got that yeast together, and we are *still* running on that same
strain that he picked up. And it's more than 60 years old now."

There are 38 fermenting tanks, ranging in size up to 70,000 gallons. As the cypress tanks gradually rotted, they have been replaced
with stainless steel.

The Vendome stills are stainless steel on the bottom portion,
but give way to copper in the head section. From the top of the
column, the vapor goes through a heat exchanger, warming up the
beer entering the still and cooling itself down into a liquid. It then
enters the 'thumper'—as the moonshiners call it—which acts as a
kind of double distillation. Out of the doubler and then through a
condenser cooled by water, the white dog finally emerges, crystal
clear, at around 125 proof.

Beam Bourbons go into the barrel at around 125 proof, and the
barrels are then moved to the warehouses.

Most of the Beam warehouses are the traditional, open-rick design, holding around 20,000 barrels. But the open-rick warehouses are rather labor-intensive. According to Booker, in an open-rick warehouse, the average workman can move seven or eight barrels per man-hour. And Beam still insists upon some rotation of the barrels; so those on the uppermost floors are moved to the bottom. For barrels aged entirely on the top floor would age very quickly, rising to perhaps 140 proof, and turning a dark, inky brown, whereas those aged only on the bottom floor would be weak in color and taste, somewhat astringent, and would actually lower in alcoholic content to maybe 110 proof.

As a means of reducing that labor, Beam has invested in a couple of palletized warehouses, where in what looks like an airplane hangar, the barrels are placed on end, nine to a pallet, and stacked pallet upon pallet. In such a warehouse, the workmen can move somewhere between 20 to 30 barrels per man-hour. Standing in such a warehouse is an experience not to be forgotten. For without the timber framing of the traditional open rick warehouse to obstruct the view, one can see perhaps 42,000 barrels at one time.

For some reason the Bourbon ages around 20 percent more slowly in these palletized warehouses. But Booker and Baker don't let that worry them; they simply let the Bourbon age a bit longer, until it is just right.

What counts as 'just right' depends upon what bottle the spirit is headed for. American Brands, James B. Beam Distilling Company's corporate parent, in 1987 acquired what was National Distillers in Frankfort. Hence, the old National Distillers' line, including Old Crow, Old Taylor, and Old Grand-Dad are now part of the extended Beam family.

Under the Beam brand name, there are four varieties that are widely available: The white label Jim Beam is 80 proof and four to four and a half years old. A green label version, usually at 86 proof is five to six years old. The black label version is 90 proof, and is aged for eight years. There is also a Jim Beam Rye Whiskey, which comes in a yellow label.

Booker, however, is most proud of the Jim Beam 'small batch' Bourbons. Noting the marketing success of single-malt Scotch

Inside the innovative palletized warehouse at Jim Beam

Mark Waymack

whiskeys, Booker was convinced that the American public was ready, indeed eager, for more traditional Bourbon, super-high quality Bourbon, made right and aged long, like they did before Prohibition.

The results are the four small-batch Bourbons: Baker's, Basil Hayden's, Knob Creek, and Booker's. The Basil Hayden and Knob Creek share the same high-rye formula, while the Baker's and Booker's share the standard Beam formula. What differentiates these products from the regular label products are three things. First, the barrels selected are allocated to the most promising warehouse locations. Second, the small-batch Bourbons are allowed to age longer than the usual bottled goods. For a variety of reasons (including national tastes as well as economics), Bourbon produced in the years after Prohibition tended to be lighter and aged less long than those made prior to Prohibition. But with an emerging market of people who are willing to pay a bit extra to get a richer tasting, smoother

Bourbon, the Beam folks decided that the small-batch Bourbons would be aged longer than is typical in these days. Finally, the small-batch Bourbons tend to be a higher proof than your run-of-the-mill Bourbon, yielding more intense flavors.

The small-batch Bourbons are more expensive than the regular Jim Beam labels, for understandable reasons. First, they tend to be aged longer, entailing additional storage costs as well as additional loss to evaporation. And second, there is a limited supply. If you skim all the cream, you are left with skim milk. Likewise, if all the cream of the barrels were bottled as small-batch, the regular Jim Beam brands would suffer. Hence, Beam must tightly limit how much they can put aside for the small-batch labels. Beam small-batch Bourbon is, therefore, a very limited-supply product.

Basil Hayden, named apparently after an early Kentucky distiller, operating in the late 1700s, is aged for eight years, and bottled at 80 proof.

Knob Creek is named for the nearby town where Thomas Lincoln (Abraham's father) owned a farm and worked at a local distillery. It is aged for nine years, and is bottled at 100 proof. The nine years in the barrel convey a dark, rich, amber-brown color. And the 100 proof give this Bourbon a remarkable substance.

Baker's, named for the retired Master Distiller, is aged for seven years, and is bottled at 107 proof.

But the Bourbon of which Booker is most proud, not surprisingly, is Booker's. It began several years ago with someone asking Booker what his favorite drink was. Thinking about it, he decided that what he really liked best was the way the Bourbon tasted straight out of the barrel, especially a good barrel that had been aged longer than usual. But while it might be a legitimate prerogative of a Master Distiller to taste what's in the barrel, as a necessary part of quality control, federal law did not look kindly upon just taking some out of the barrel and selling to other people.

Happily, this is now a legal possibility. So Booker can now choose some of the best barrels in the warehouse—typically found in the heart of a traditional warehouse. These barrels are allowed to age somewhere between six and eight years, depending upon Booker's judgment. When deemed ready, they are dumped, and without any filtering and with no addition of water, the Bourbon is bottled. This means that labels must be customized for each batch, since the proof will vary somewhat, ranging between 123 and 126. Booker affirms, without any hesitation or doubt, "That's my favorite drink. Truly uncut, unfiltered, straight from the barrel. Straight from the barrel is the way they did it a hundred years ago, the way my grand-daddy did it. They didn't go through all this chilling and filtering. And when you chill, filter, and add that charcoal to it, you are tak-ing out some of the original flavors—you knock some of the barrel taste out of it. I'm not trying to sell you a bill of goods. Booker's Bourbon has absolutely nothing done to it. That's the way I like it."

Booker's Bourbon is indeed a unique product. As you hold the bottle up to the light, noting the beautiful amber color gleaned from years in the charred barrel, you can occasionally even see small flecks of the char swimming ever so lazily in the bottle. When you uncork the bottle, rich barrel aromas entice you—oaky, char aro-mas you cannot find in any other Bourbon that we have come across. And be forewarned that 125 proof is *serious* stuff! Knowledgeable drinkers tend to add a small splash of pure, unchlorinated spring water to help release the aromas and flavors packed into this re-markable Bourbon.

Booker knows Bourbon. As an easily affordable Bourbon, Jim Beam white label is an industry leader. As a small-batch producer, the James B. Beam Distilling Company is a high-quality innovator. And as the producer of Booker's, the Beam Company thus far stands in a class by itself.

TASTING NOTES

Jim Beam White Label, 40 percent, 4 years
A light amber color. Distinctly floral aroma. On the palate it is light- to medium-bodied, with identifiable vanilla, though a bit lacking in depth, with a rapidly fading finish.

Jim Beam Green Label, 43 percent, 5 years
Slightly darker than the four-year-old, this still offers a simi-

lar flowery nose (some ethyl acetate?). Between the extra year and the marginally higher proof, there is a bit more depth on the palate. This label has recently been discontinued.

Jim Beam Black Label, 45 percent, 8 years
A good amber color. The nose is flowery with a hint of sweetness. The body is full, with characteristic vanilla notes. Noticeably richer than the four- or five-year, but lacking the depth of the small-batch line.

Old Grand-Dad, 40 percent
A medium bodied whiskey. The rye content is evident, though one would not call it coarse.

Old Grand-Dad 114, 57 percent
The high proof definitely makes this a more intense experience than the regular strength Old Grand-Dad. A good, warm nose, with oaky tones. On the palate, it is medium-bodied, balanced, and tending to the dry side. A high rye content is evident in its reedy texture. Some barrel notes, but a small splash of water brought them out a little better. Hints of vanilla and caramel, but certainly not a sweet Bourbon.

Basil Hayden, 40 percent, 8 years
The amber color is evidence of the years in the wood. The nose is complex but subtle, with the smoky wood tones of the Bourbon barrel char. The high proportion of small grains is evident in a full-bodied, relatively dry flavor. The low proof keeps the whiskey from being heavy or oily. There is a lingering finish, where the rye becomes most noticeable.

Knob Creek, 50 percent, 9 years
The color is rich and dark, the extra year and the higher proof combining to produce a much darker whiskey than the Basil Hayden. The nose is dense, loaded with wood and caramel-toffee tones. The 100 proof gives the palate not only a denser, richer taste, but also a heavier texture. Once again, a high small grains content is noticeable in the relatively

dry taste and finish. Taken straight from the bottle, you almost feel like chewing it. This is a truly fine sipping whiskey.

Baker's, 53.5 percent, 7 years

This is distinguished from the Booker's by a specified age, a lower alcohol content, a filtering process when it comes out of the barrel, and a lower price tag. Mellow, rich, and sweet. The color is a warm amber, evidence of the #4 char in the Beam barrels. There is more floweriness (some ethyl acetate?) and a more noticeable sweetness (because of the high corn content) than in the Basil Hayden or Knob Creek. At 107 proof (seven degrees 'over-proof'), the whiskey has a delightful heaviness, an oily viscosity that rings the glass with a shimmering bead. On the palate it has that distinctive vanilla-caramel sweetness of Bourbon, but is certainly not cloying. An uplifting experience, not to be missed.

Booker's, 61.5 percent–63 percent, 6–8 years

This Bourbon is in a class by itself. It is currently the only Bourbon sold uncut and unfiltered, just as it comes out of the barrel. The color is a beautiful honey-amber. The nose is rich in woody, char barrel notes, and adding a splash of spring water (or distilled water—stay away from chlorinated tap water if you can) releases even more aroma. The exquisite taste is about as full and complex as a Bourbon gets. Try a sip straight from the bottle at barrel proof; then cut it with pure water to about 100 proof. Even some clean ice can be used without masking the depth of this Bourbon. A work of genius. A Revelation.

VISITING

The Jim Beam plant at Clermont is well-equipped for visitors. From Route 65, south of Louisville, take exit 112 (Bardstown/Bernheim Forest) to Highway 245. Turn east and go one and a half miles to "Jim Beam's American Outpost." A tour includes an informative video, a warehouse visit, an exhibit on barrel-making, another with an early copper 'moonshiner's' still, and a well-stocked gift shop.

The distillery is open for visitors Mondays through Saturdays 9:00 A.M.–4:30 P.M., and Sundays 1:00 P.M.–4:00 P.M.

Leestown Distilling
Company, Inc.

Leestown Distilling, the home of Ancient Age, Blanton's, Rock Hill Farm, Elmer T. Lee, and Hancock's Reserve, stands as a success story, based upon such all-American virtues as quality, adaptability, skill, and timely innovation.

Leestown, one of the earliest settlements in Kentucky, is not far from Frankfort, a couple of miles or so. The sprawl of the state capital has long since over-run the old town. Hence, our spirits tended to flag as we followed our directions to the distillery, driving down a busy thoroughfare lined with strip malls, hotels, and fast food establishments.

Appearances, as any philosopher knows, can be deceiving, but the trained eye can see things to which the uninitiated are oblivious.

In an unpublished manuscript from the 1950s, pertaining to the history of distilling at this site, Colonel Albert B. Blanton writes:

> The State of Kentucky once published an official Geological Map, authenticated by complete surveys, and showing the various strata that outcrop upon the surface and from the soil bed. This map shows that in the small section of the State, made World Famous by its fine sour mash whiskeys, the rare bird's eye limestone of the lowest stratum of the Lower Silurian formation alone outcrops. This small section, with the exception of a small isolated strip in Powell's Valley in Southwest Virginia and East Tennessee, is solitary in the one remarkable geological feature in the whole West. The whiskey manufactured at this plant [Where Leestown Distilling now stands and operates] is produced upon the depressed apex of this stratum, thus securing the best limestone drainage it can possibly afford. The result in fine whiskey is, no doubt, largely due to the water that percolating through the limestone becomes impregnated with its properties, and imparts them to the spirit during the process of manufacture. Opinions and assertions are

debatable—a geological fact, stereotyped in the reflected form of the earth's crystallized strata, is as solid and immovable as the everlasting hills. (From 'The Geo. T. Stagg Company, Leestown,' by Albert B. Blanton, ca. 1950)

Whatever it is, however it is, things seem to work well here, for the Leestown products—Ancient Age, Ancient Ancient Age, Rock Hill Farms, Hancock's Reserve, Elmer T. Lee, and especially Blanton's—are truly fine Bourbons, as demonstrated by their outstanding performance in Bourbon tastings.

Once you turn off of the highway (look for the large Ancient Age sign) and head onto the distillery property, leaving the traffic and strip malls behind, things change for the better. High on a hill, overlooking the landscape, is the 'Landmark Building,' erected in 1776. It has been exquisitely maintained and refurbished and now serves as administrative offices. Down the hill (and we do mean *down*), setting on the banks of the majestic Kentucky River, are the distillery premises, made of brick and clearly intended to last for a long time.

The site is well chosen. A reliable, high-volume spring of limestone water, rich in calcium carbonate and calcium phosphate, is quite near. In addition to this spring, known as the O.F.C. Spring, after the 'Old Fashioned Copper Distillery,' the site also has access to the 'Cove Spring,' an abundant source discovered in 1773. The Kentucky River provided both navigable access and, quite likely, cooling water for the distillery operations.

Distilling seems to have begun perhaps in the 1860s, with Ben H. Blanton (father of the famous Colonel Albert B. Blanton) as owner and distiller. It is unclear exactly what happened next. Perhaps the Civil War spelled a demise for the Blanton enterprise, but it appears as if Blanton sold off the land into small farm parcels.

Then, in 1869–70, the owners of those parcels of land sold them, along with the existing and apparently disused distillery buildings and equipment, to E. H. Taylor. Taylor seems to have learned distilling at the Old Oscar Pepper and Old Crow distilleries before deciding to launch out into his own enterprise. He refurbished the exist-

*Watertower
of Leestown
Distilling,
home of
Ancient Age*

Mark Waymack

ing plant and named it the 'O.F.C.,' standing apparently for 'Old Fashioned Copper Distillery.' In 1873, Captain George T. Stagg entered the picture. A corporation was formed under the name of 'E.H. Taylor, Jr. Company.' Stagg was the principal owner, while Taylor became the manager. From here the story gets quite complicated for a while, with ownership of several properties or interests passing between Taylor and Stagg, along with a long trail of litigation between the two. At least we know that in 1886, Stagg became sole owner, and the plant was renamed the 'George T. Stagg Distillery.' And we know that in 1897, Stagg hired Albert B. Blanton. Blanton rose to the rank of distillery manager in 1912, and continued in that capacity until his retirement in 1952.

While the distillery did not produce whiskey during Prohibition, it did serve as a collection warehouse and bottler of medicinal whiskey. In 1929, Schenley purchased the facility, perhaps anticipating the eventual repeal of Prohibition. Production of Bourbon was resumed in 1933.

Schenley invested in a great deal of modernization and expansion around 1940. While the production of Bourbon was curtailed during the War, the distillery did produce some 42 million gallons of alcohol for the U.S. Government as part of the war effort. The Ancient Age brand made its debut as a Bourbon in 1946, and as a result of its great success in the market, the name of the distillery was, in 1969, changed from the 'Schenley Distillery' to 'Ancient Age Distilling Company.' Since 1992, it has operated independently under the name, 'Leestown Distilling Company, Inc.,' though its president also serves as president of the large whiskey firm, Sazerac.

Having been quite successful in the heyday of Bourbon, the plant is quite large. A long history of producing Bourbon saw the distillery's five millionth barrel filled in 1982, which now stands in a miniature warehouse all to itself. And the plant is capable of mashing some two million bushels of grain per year—meaning a potential yield of ten million proof gallons annually. Such busy days, are in the past, though a growing appreciation of fine whiskey may one day bring them back. When we visited, the plant was using far less than full capacity, with several of the enormous cookers and fermenters not having been used for years. In recent years the plant has been running about eight months of the year, producing at slightly more than one-third of its daily capacity.

The formula (and there is only one for all the different Bourbons produced by the distillery), by repute, is high in corn—just under 80 percent (which is pressure cooked to maximize potential yield)—with the remainder being split between malted barley and rye.

The bulk of Leestown's Bourbon is bottled as Ancient Age, or at ten years old as Ancient Ancient Age. These are definitely solid,

Gary Gayheart, Master Distiller at Leestown, supervising the controls for the beer still

Mark Waymack

well-made, mainstream Bourbons. But what distinguishes Leestown is its position as the originator of 'single-barrel' Bourbons. Leestown confronted the lessened demand for 'brown spirits' in its own innovative way. Observing the phenomenal demand for single-malt Scotch whiskies—where consumers have displayed a willingness, even an eagerness, to pay more for an exceptionally high-quality product—Leestown developed the notion of a 'single-barrel Bourbon.' It offers four single-barrel Bourbons: 'Blanton's,' 'Rock Hill Farm,' 'Elmer T. Lee,' and 'Hancock's Reserve.'

Elmer T. Lee perhaps deserves the title of Master Distiller Emeritus. He began working at the distillery as an engineer in 1949, was promoted to plant superintendent in 1964, and to manager in 1968. Thus, he began work under Colonel Blanton. Apparently, it was Lee's idea to bottle a single-barrel Bourbon, and also his idea to name that label 'Blanton's,' in honor of the Colonel. Production began in 1984.

Now, with respect to Scottish whiskies, the term 'single' has come to mean that the whisky in the bottle comes entirely from one distillery. It has not been blended with the whisky of any other distillery.

American whiskey producers couldn't simply adopt the Scots terminology, since virtually all 'straight' whiskeys would qualify as 'single' in this sense. 'Single Bourbon,' therefore, by itself would not mean anything special.

What Lee came up with is the notion of a 'single-*barrel* Bourbon.' The basic idea is that Elmer T. Lee periodically checks the warehouses, keeping an eye (and nose) out for exceptionally good barrels—what Lee calls 'sugar barrels.' These barrels are collected in Warehouse H, the warehouse that Lee believes offers the best aging conditions. Leestown, unlike most distilleries, heats its warehouses in the winter to maintain a minimum of 40 degrees Fahrenheit. According to Joe Darmand, vice president, "We're one of the few who heat our warehouses. It costs somewhere around $200,000 a year to do that, but we think it makes a better Bourbon." Periodic testing continues, and when Lee determines that a barrel is ready, it is transported to a building reserved for Blanton's. This small, squarish building used to be the railroad station on the premises, when most supplies came in by rail and finished whiskey was shipped out by rail. There, unmixed with any other barrels—Blanton's or otherwise—the single barrel is dumped, filtered, and cut with pure water to 93 proof. A slew of workers then fill the bottles by hand, prepare the labels with the date of dumping and the number of the barrel, glue on the label by hand, insert the cork with the trademark horse and jockey on top by hand, apply the gold sealing wax by hand, place the bottle in its unique velveteen bag by hand, and pack it in a cardboard case box by hand. In all our visits to American whiskey distilleries, we have never seen anything else that comes close to this labor-intensive handling. As Darmand put it, "There are twenty-two people there, producing 220 cases a day." The effort seems to pay off. Blanton's has done consistently well in Bourbon tastings. And with the upscale packaging holding a superior quality

Mark Waymack

The Kentucky River at Leestown

Bourbon, sales have been strong. Not only has Blanton's been successful here at home, it is also strong in the European market, especially Germany. Japan is the largest export market of all. Total export sales of Blanton's are larger than domestic sales.

Elmer Lee also selects those barrels that go into the Elmer T. Lee bottles. The major differences between this and the Blanton's label would appear to be age (we think the Elmer T. Lee brand is a bit younger than the Blanton's) and the proof (the Elmer T. Lee is bottled at a marginally lower alcoholic strength than Blanton's).

The general idea behind Rock Hill Farm and Hancock's Reserve, the other single-barrel Bourbons produced at Leestown, is pretty much the same as Blanton's, except that it is master distiller Gary Gayheart who chooses the barrels. Gayheart brings no shortage of experience or skill to this task, having been the master distiller here since 1969.

As we walked around the distillery, accompanied by Gayheart, we asked him just what qualities he hopes to produce in a barrel of Leestown Bourbon. He points out that in general terms there are four things that make the Leestown products distinctive: First is the limestone-rich water, with the distillery's water drawn mostly from underground, limestone sources. Second is the formula, high in corn. Third is the strain of yeast, a strain which, he insists, pro-

James Harris

Bottling Blanton's Single-Barrel Bourbon by hand

duces a distiller's beer with just the right balance of components. Fourth and last is the aging process. At Leestown they use barrels with a #3 char.

It seems far more difficult, though, to put into words exactly what Gayheart is looking for in a particular barrel in order to deem it appropriate for the Rock Hill Farms or Hancock's Reserve labels. He can say only: "It's a personal taste . . . hard to describe. I'm looking for those that have the taste that impresses me the most."

The term 'sugar barrel' is helpful, for it reflects our sense that what Lee and Gayheart both value highly are a certain strong sweetness, along with a full, mellow body, lacking in harshness, qualities that tend to be enhanced by aging in the 'heart' of the warehouse.

The single-barrel phenomenon owes something to marketing hype, no doubt. But it is based on substance. The wise consumer understands that single-barrel bottlings are subject to variability, and that some of what they are paying for is packaging. But the undeniable truth remains that these are unusually fine Bourbons. The discriminating imbiber owes a tip of the hat to Leestown—to Elmer T. Lee and Gary Gayheart—for raising the ante in the Bourbon industry and forcing others to compete by developing their own select whiskeys.

TASTING NOTES

The house style of Leestown is definitely in the sweetest tradition of Bourbon. The high percentage of corn contributes to this. But it is also undoubtedly emphasized by warehousing practices. Like it or not, and not everyone does, these Bourbons are at the sweet end of the spectrum. It is by no accident then, that the barrels chosen for the various single-barrel Bourbons here are called 'sugar barrels.'

As regards the four single-barrel Bourbons produced here, they are high-quality Bourbons, and clearly in the sweet tradition. We confess that when pure water was used to bring them to the same proof, it was difficult for us to discriminate reliably between Leestown's four different single-barrel labels. This was especially noticeable since we tried to compare not only the different labels, but also different barrels within the same label.

If you like your Bourbon sweet, then you really should try one or more of these single-barrel Bourbons from Leestown.

Ancient Age, 40 percent
A light, but fragrant nose. On the sweet side. Medium-bodied in the mouth, it rolls around and releases a sweet center, leaning in the vanilla direction. Noticeable barrel notes of light char. A decent finish.

Ancient Ancient Age, 40 percent
Quite similar to Ancient Age. The barrel char is a bit more muted. And the sweetness is a bit deeper, less on the surface. A long, pleasant finish.

Blanton's, 46.5 percent
This is a remarkable Bourbon. Indeed, it could be said to define a particular Bourbon style. It begins with a rich, sweet aroma, with hints of caramel and char in it. Then, in the mouth it is medium-bodied, but yet also full, smooth, and rounded. It is distinctively sweet, encompassing the sweetness of the corn as well as the vanilla and caramel sweetness from the charred barrel. The finish is long, smooth, and, yes, sweet.

Rock Hill Farm, 50 percent

A light, sweet aroma. It rolls around in the mouth, offering hints of toffee. It is medium-to-full bodied, smooth, rounded, and quite sweet. The finish is also long and sweet.

Hancock's Reserve, 44.5 percent

A light, but pleasant nose, with noticeable sweetness. Medium bodied, with a mellow, vanilla sweetness. A characteristically long finish, with vanilla and caramel.

Elmer T. Lee, 45 percent

Light, fragrant aroma, with some vanilla in it. On the palate, it is full, round, and sweet. Vanilla is prominent, with caramel in the background. The finish is sweet and lingering.

VISITING

Leestown Distilling has a well-equipped, instructive, and quite pleasant Visitor Center on the premises. There is an informative video, a tour, and a well-stocked gift and souvenir shop. For information on visiting hours or tours, call 502-223-7641.

Maker's Mark

Maker's Mark Bourbon, produced at the Star Hill Distillery, also known as the Maker's Mark Distillery, represents an unusual melding of tradition and innovation. In some ways rooted, almost reverentially, in the past, Maker's Mark is also in some ways an innovator, indeed, a tradition-breaker. T. William Samuels, Jr., president of Maker's Mark, would argue that to make a really fine Bourbon, the best one can, one must learn not to be a slave of the past. Rather, one should understand the past, appreciate the past, know what is important to preserve of the past, yet learn how the tradition should be altered for the better.

The Samuels family has been in Kentucky for seven generations, and distilling whisky there just as long. (Company literature eschews the common American spelling of 'whiskey' in favor of the Scottish preference for 'whisky.') At first, the family was primarily involved in the timber industry, with whisky-making as a sideline. The Samuels family history is interwoven with some of the more colorful history of the region. One of the distant Samuelses was stepfather to Frank and Jesse James; and there are James brothers memorabilia kept at the distillery, including a set of pistols. Fortunately, the Samuelses have demonstrated more of a flair for distilling than for step-parenting. Nancy, the wife of Bill Samuels, Jr., traces her ancestry to Daniel Boone as well as to a long lineage of Boone distillers.

Taylor Williams Samuels, the current Samuelses' great-great-grandfather, seems to have been the first of the Samuelses to go into distilling as a full-time career. Born in 1821 and educated at Bardstown College, T.W. Samuels at one time served as sheriff and magistrate for Nelson County. A writer for the *Nelson County Record* describes Samuels in a "Supplement" of 1896 as being "one of the most solid business men in the county, and personally is quite an interesting and companiable gentleman, being well posted upon

historical and industrial subjects." (We can attest that this descrip-
tion of a century ago applies perfectly to Bill Samuels, Jr.) The *Nelson
Record* goes on to note that Samuels's distillery, constructed in
Deatsville in 1844,

> is well constructed, and equipped with all the modern improvements
> known in the distillery business. He uses the most select grain and has
> as his distiller one of the best and most popular men engaged in the
> business. The warehouses are well arranged and perfectly ventilated
> and are iron-clad. Whisky generally is entered at a per cent of 101 proof,
> and when it is due for withdrawal has reached as high as 109. The
> average increase, though, is about four or five degrees, which speaks
> well for the maturing advantages to be obtained at this distillery. . . . it
> has a daily capacity of two hundred and fifteen bushels of grain. The
> warehouses have a capacity of over 14,000 barrels.

It was T. William Samuels, Sr., though, who took the bold step
that led to the Star Hill distillery and the Maker's Mark brand. T.W.
Samuels, Sr., was no stranger to distilling. When Prohibition ended,
he had helped to rehabilitate the old T.W. Samuels distillery in
Deatsville, where he served as vice president and general manager.
But the distillery had been sold in 1943, and when Samuels returned
from the War, it was closed. The year was 1953, a time of relative
glut in the industry, and Taylor William Samuels, Sr. was finding
his post-World War II career unfulfilling. Selling timber, contract-
ing, selling machinery, just didn't satisfy him. Rather than heed pre-
vailing wisdom, he purchased a disused, dilapidated distillery in
Loretto, the Happy Hollow Distillery.

Samuels's idea was that while there might be a glut of unwanted,
old-fashioned whiskey, there was an unmet demand for a different
kind of Bourbon—something less coarse, less harsh, and more
mellow. Borrowing from the experience of the Old Fitzgerald brand
in Louisville, Samuels decided that, by using winter wheat instead
of the coarser-tasting rye, he could produce a more mellow, softer,
yet still full-flavored Bourbon whiskey. Not only did he choose a
non-traditional grain mixture, but he also insisted upon a longer
maturation period than was typical in the industry at that time—
requiring six years in his refurbished, traditional, open-rick warehouses. Using the traditional though labor-intensive method of

*Bill Samuels,
President of
Maker's Mark,
at the copper
tailboxes,
where the
spirit comes
off the still*

Mark Waymack

rotating barrels about the warehouse as they age, he was able to ensure a consistently well-aged final product.

At the time, the Samuels family lived in Bardstown, next door neighbors to Jim Beam and across the street from Jack Beam. Amidst a warm friendship, who knows what kind of helpful advice this clan of men on 'Distillers' Row' gave to Samuels? Not surprisingly, when Samuels went looking for advice and counsel he chose from a family of long distilling experience, the Beams, Elmo Beam. He then recruited Samuel Kenneth Cecil as his master distiller, who finally retired around 1980. The current master distiller is Steve Nally, who has been with Maker's Mark for 22 years. The first Maker's Mark went to market in 1959, and since then there has been no looking back, with output expanding each year.

In 1981, Samuels, Sr., sold the distillery; it is now owned by the Hiram Walker corporation. However, it still retains much of a family flavor with Taylor William Samuels, Jr., as president. While T.W. Samuels, Sr. must be credited with creating Maker's Mark, it is Bill Samuels, Jr., who has combined so successfully Bourbon-making wisdom with a real marketing flair.

Other distillers seem to regard Bill Samuels, Jr., as something of a maverick, but they all do so with respect, for no one we met denied Samuels's remarkable talents. Tall, lean and energetic, Bill Samuels is at the forefront of promoting Bourbon, and in particular Maker's Mark, in the international market. Indeed, it was sometimes difficult for us to catch up with him, as he was either off in Germany or somewhere on the Pacific Rim, preaching the virtues of Maker's Mark and Kentucky Bourbon.

As one long-time distiller explained to us: "Bill Samuels can take a thought or idea and put it into an ad. He'll take this ad and do things that are unconventional with it. For example, one came out recently about two people who kept breaking into a liquor store in Florida, and the *only* thing they would do is steal the Maker's Mark. So the liquor store owner no longer carries Maker's Mark, for fear these people will break into his store and try to steal it. Bill can get just the right twist on this, so that what you come away thinking is just how desirable Maker's Mark is."

Our visit to Maker's Mark began with David Salmon picking us up in Bardstown and driving us south, through some beautiful, rolling countryside, to what is reputed to be the smallest (legal) operational distillery in the United States.

As we drove up to the distillery, the first thing that struck us was just how architecturally charming the place is. Indeed, as we discovered, the distillery has been designated as a National and Kentucky Historic Landmark structure. (We also later learned that T. Williams Samuels, Jr., has himself been quite active in efforts to preserve the architectural heritage of the Kentucky countryside.)

Like any whiskey, Maker's Mark begins with grain. In this case, as noted, it is corn, winter wheat, and malted barley. Only top quality grain is used, of course. All of it is drawn from as close by as is practical. Some of it even comes from the farmland of the nearby

Roman Catholic convent, the Laurentine Sisters of Loretto. The proportions, about which Maker's Mark makes no secret, are around 70 percent corn, 14 percent winter wheat, and 16 percent malted barley.

As we toured the distillery, Salmon pointed out the grain mill. The grain is crushed in an old-fashioned roller mill, rather than in the hammer mills that became common in the 1950s and 1960s. While there have been advances in the technology of hammer mills, Maker's Mark still believes that the roller mills are gentler to the grains.

The cooking is done at a relatively low temperature for up to four hours, in order to be 'gentle' to the grain. This is especially necessary because wheat requires a lower cooking temperature than does rye. The mashing is straightforward and typical, and as the mash enters the fermenters it is mixed with a one-third portion of setback, a remarkably high percentage.

It was in the fermenting room where our attention really began to perk up. All of the fermenters, every last one of them, each holding approximately 9,600 gallons, are made of cypress. There is not a stainless steel one in the bunch. Painstaking maintenance is the rule, for repairs are increasingly difficult, and replacement is inconceivable—not just because of expense, but more so because of lack of skilled craftsmen in the field. Maintaining cypress tanks is a dying art-form and a serious commitment to the past.

Several of the vats were fermenting vigorously while we were visiting; and one was being cleaned, its distiller's beer having just been pumped over to the still. The workmen hosing down the sides noticed our rapt attention, which prompted a story:

A few years ago, a fairly well-known British journalist and photographer made a visit, perhaps because of the Glenmorangie connection which we shall explain in a bit. He, too, was impressed by the cypress vats, and like us he had a hard time figuring how to capture a sense of their depth on film. Unlike us, however, he had the not-so-bright idea of climbing down into a freshly-emptied vat and taking a picture looking up.

The distillery staff, in their polite Kentucky style, suggested that this might not be the swiftest of notions, but the fellow insisted. So, a ladder was found and lowered into the vat, and the intrepid photographer climbed down.

Now, as we have had occasion to explain, the two most noticeable by-products of fermentation are alcohol and carbon dioxide— *lots* of carbon dioxide. If you stick your head over a fermenting vat and keep it there for long, you become woozy from lack of oxygen. *And,* carbon dioxide, being a relatively heavy gas, tends to settle in the lower air pockets until it is entirely mixed with the rest of the surrounding atmosphere.

So, when this enterprising photographer reached the bottom of the ladder and stood upon the floor of the fermenter, he had entered a world that might have offered a remarkable photograph, if he could have retained consciousness long enough, but also one that was rich in carbon dioxide and quite poor in oxygen. So, he promptly keeled over.

Figuring that this would likely happen, the staff was prepared. One worker donned the equivalent of a scuba tank, climbed down and carried the limp form of the photographer up. The use of oxygen readily saved the day, though, the sought-after photograph was never taken.

Needless to say, we were not at all tempted to repeat such a remarkable event, even if it might have provided the Maker's Mark staff with more humorous anecdotal material about the foibles of writers and photographers to share with future visitors to the distillery.

Does cypress, rather than stainless steel, really make a difference in the end? We doubt it. Even Bill Samuels expressed some skepticism in a later conversation; but, he noted, the distillery workers regard the cypress vats with a good deal of respect, perhaps even superstitious awe. And who knows? So, tradition has a place, and if it does no harm, and perhaps does some bit of good, why not maintain it? Besides, making whiskey is more than simply an exercise in science or efficiency.

From the fermenting room we progressed to the still. Like virtually every (legal) still in operation in Kentucky, this one is made by Vendome. Unlike many, however, it is cleaned and polished to a remarkable, reflective gleam.

The crafted, polished copper and glass 'tail boxes,' where the distiller can check the temperature and proof of the whisky as it comes off the still, maintaining a sharp eye on quality, are truly works of art. These tail boxes are justifiably one of the many points of pride at Maker's Mark. Another unusual feature of Maker's Mark is its doubler. Instead of the usual contraption called a 'thumper,' the doubler here is essentially a pot still. As Samuels tells it, "We didn't start out with a pot still. We started with a funny looking contraption. And my father had a friend of his over from Scotland. They got to fiddling around and made the change back in the beginning of Maker's Mark to the pot."

From approximately 5 percent alcohol in the fermenters, the white dog comes out of the doubler at around 65 percent, or 130 proof. It then goes into the barrel at 109–110 proof.

As we walked from the still to the cistern room, we noticed a couple of metal pails, each nearly full of what looks like a gritty black powder with a small handful of a white powder thrown on top. Though we have visited many distilleries, this is something we had never seen before, or since. We asked one of the workmen and we got the beginning of an answer:

"Oh, those? Yeah, they go in the dog before it goes to the barrels."

We started to develop a hunch, a hunch that we later tested over lunch with Bill Samuels. Samuels straightforwardly explained that the stuff is mostly carbon, ground pure charcoal, that is stirred into the spirit as it collects in the cistern. Its purpose is to act as a kind of filter, like an activated charcoal filter. The carbon absorbs some of the more volatile and (at least in the Maker's Mark philosophy) undesirable congeners. One can certainly notice a remarkable difference between the white dog as it comes straight off the still, and the spirit after the carbon treatment, just prior to being barrelled. Many of the coarser grain notes and highlights are subdued or entirely gone, and a mellowness, with rounded edges, is already present—effects that are in keeping with Maker's Mark's intentions.

Perhaps we were simply not observant enough, but we never saw this done at any other Bourbon distillery, though a quite different charcoal 'mellowing' is an essential, indeed *defining*, part of the

Tennessee Whiskey process. The filtering is clearly a strategy in harmony with the Maker's Mark ideal of a light, soft, yet full-in-the-middle kind of Bourbon whiskey.

In yet another Maker's Mark singularity, the barrel bungs are walnut, whereas everywhere else they use poplar for the bung. The argument is that at Maker's Mark they do a *lot* of taste-testing of the spirit as it ages. So to maintain accessibility as well as good sealing, they lay a small square of burlap over the bung hole and then hammer in the walnut bung. The burlap provides the repeated access and the walnut, a denser, stronger wood than poplar, provides the durability and sealing strength.

Another idiosyncrasy at Maker's Mark is their insistence upon an extra year of air drying for their barrel wood over the industry norm. This is because of a concern that any green wood in a barrel stave could detract from the quality of that barrel's Bourbon.

Aging is done in open-rick warehouses. In the self-conscious, and aesthetically attractive Maker's Mark style, the warehouses are painted a distinctive black, with bright red shutters, each carved with the shape of the Maker's Mark bottle.

Moving filled 53-gallon barrels about, especially by hand, is time-consuming and labor-intensive. Some whiskey distilleries have either moved to cavernous large warehouses, where large blocks of barrels are stacked on pallets and left, or else they maintain the open-rick warehouses, but do not rotate the stock. This means that different barrels, left in different parts of the warehouse, age differently. Those at the top, where it is hottest, age most quickly. Those at the very bottom age much more slowly. Those at the periphery are subject to violent extremes—heat in the summer and cold in the winter. So to achieve a pleasing whiskey for the bottle, the distiller dumps a large number of barrels—perhaps hundreds—at once, allowing the whiskey to mingle for a short while before bottling.

At Maker's Mark, however, Samuels emphasizes with pride that, though it is expensive and labor-intensive, the barrels are rotated in the warehouse. Freshly filled barrels are started on the top floors, and then gradually moved down to the more temperate sections of the warehouse, until the aging has reached just the right point, which is still around six years. This way, each barrel dumped should be of

Maker's Mark Distillery, a National Registered Historic Landmark

the same high quality as every other barrel. Of course, if you are going to move barrels around, then you must have some place to which to move them. So Maker's Mark has to keep its warehouses about 25 percent empty. By a remarkable connection, the Maker's Mark formula and the care and, attention they devote to their warehousing benefit not only the Bourbon aficionado. While Bourbon benefits from being aged in new, charred oak barrels—indeed, that is one distinctive and legally required part of making Bourbon— Scotch whisky benefits from longer aging in much less assertive wood. So the preference in Scotland runs toward used barrels— used sherry barrels or, increasingly, used Bourbon barrels. Glenmorangie, a Scottish malt distillery of high repute, located in the north on the Firth of Tain, after years of experimenting chose to acquire its barrels from Maker's Mark. So, whenever you take a glass of Glenmorangie (the 18-year-old is truly magnificent), you are also benefitting from the care and skill of Bill Samuels and the Maker's Mark Distillery.

Ever curious (an engineer by education, as well as a lawyer), Samuels has long been intrigued about the differing aging conditions between Kentucky and northern Scotland. So, in a tantalizing experiment, a barrel of Glenmorangie now rests in a Maker's Mark warehouse, alongside barrel after barrel of Bourbon. And unlike aging in the cool, damp Highlands of Scotland, this barrel of Glenmorangie has been gaining in alcoholic proof each summer it spends in Kentucky. How we envy the lucky people who will have a chance to sample this Kentucky-aged single malt Scotch alongside a dram taken from a sister Glenmorangie barrel in the warehouse in Tain.

When wood, time and temperature have done their work, the barrels are dumped, and the whisky is charcoal filtered and cut with spring water to bring it from around 113 proof down to the appropriate bottling proof. Unlike other distilleries, Maker's Mark chooses *not* to chill-filter. Their argument is that chill-filtering's only purpose is to prevent haze from later developing in the spirit. It does not benefit the flavor; indeed, it strips out some of the desirable congengers. Furthermore, as Bill Samuels argues, their water is so pure to start with that chill-hazing is not a problem for Maker's Mark.

The distinctively shaped Maker's Mark bottles are filled, capped, and labelled. Then, in a manner peculiar to Maker's Mark, each bottle is hand-dipped in a unique red sealing wax. Gold wax is used for Maker's Mark Limited Edition, a special bottling at a slightly higher alcoholic proof. This seems to be an innovation introduced by Bill Samuels, Jr., and we think it is an excellent one. On occasion, Bill Samuels has arranged for bottles to be dipped in the color of the University of Kentucky (though his own alma mater is Case-Western Reserve). One can sometimes even spy the distinctive, squarish Maker's Mark bottle with a *green* wax seal, sometimes used to designate pre-mixed Maker's Mark mint julep.

The company's name and trademark were developed by T.W. Samuels, Sr., and his wife. As the story goes, when Mr. Samuels, Sr. was getting into production, he decided he wanted to get his wife involved as well. They worked and worked on coming up with a name for the product, but nothing seemed to fit. Now, Mrs. Samuels was a collector of old English pewter, and on the bottom of all hand-made pewter and silver there is a stamp, a mark called the 'maker's mark.' She suggested that would be a good name for the whisky— Maker's Mark—because it reflected the quality and craftsmanship that her husband was putting into the product. The shape of the bottle was also her idea. She collected cognac bottles and she felt that the cognac bottle represented something people would recognize as denoting quality. As for the mark itself, the star represents Star Hill Farm; 'S' stands for the Samuels family; and the roman numeral four stands for the fourth generation of commercial distilling by the Samuels family. Finally, Mrs. Samuels was a chemist by education. Feeling that a wax seal would bespeak quality, she developed the original formula for the wax in her kitchen. Although lots of people think it is plastic, it is really a specially formulated wax.

Filling Maker's Mark miniatures, complete with the red wax seal

James Harris

Production remains small, averaging 54 barrels a day. Indeed, Maker's Mark is in some ways comparable to the 'microbreweries' that have emerged in America in recent years. This helps explain Samuels' attitude toward the single-barrel and small-batch phenomena; if you keep everything on a small scale, and pay attention to the proper maturation of each and every barrel, as at Maker's Mark, then there's nothing left that wouldn't be high-quality. As Bill Samuels says, "*Every* barrel we make is the best it can be. And if it ain't broke, don't fix it!" Truly, 'small-batch' Bourbon wouldn't make much sense at Maker's Mark, where the whole operation is small batch—compare Maker's Mark's 54 barrels per day to Beam's 1,300. While output is limited, there is no shortage of flattering accolades. A company brochure includes some selected quotations: "it's simply the best," from Claude Tattinger, of champagne fame; "The smoothest, most luxuriant Bourbon in the country is Maker's Mark," from *Esquire Magazine;* "unequivocally the finest Bourbon in the world" from the editor of *Wine Tidings.*

Critics will reply that Maker's Mark may well be excellent at what it is, but that what it is *not* is traditional Bourbon. The exceptional lightness, softness and smoothness of Maker's Mark, so appreciated by some, is achieved at the price of losing many of the more traditional flavor components of old-fashioned Bourbon. But if soft, rounded, light, and smooth are what you seek in a Bourbon, Maker's Mark has no equal.

TASTING NOTES

Maker's Mark, 45 percent
Roughly six years in the barrel, this is a very polished whisky. The absence of rye is noticeable. Smooth and light are bywords: there are no rough edges while there is still some depth. A nice, long, rounded finish.

Maker's Mark Limited Edition, 50.5 percent
A bit heavier than the red seal 45 percent, clearly showing a longer aging, both in a much darker color and in the nose and taste. Deeper barrel tones, with some toffee and a bit of a sherry note are evident. Even at a higher proof, this is not

as fiery as the red seal version Even with the longer aging, the whiskey is not woody. While the toffee or caramel notes are stronger than in the red seal, the vanilla notes, common in Bourbons, are for some reason more subdued than in the red seal version. Limited Edition is really quite an excellent Bourbon by our measure.

VISITING

Maker's Mark welcomes, encourages and is well prepared for visitors. The most difficult part of visiting will be finding the distillery. It is located in some beautiful countryside, south of Bardstown, two miles east of Loretto, off Route 52. Travel south out of Bardstown on Route 49 for 9.8 miles to the junction with Route 527. Go straight ahead (south) on 527 for 3.5 miles to Route 52. Turn left (east) on Route 52 and go through Loretto. Two miles east of Loretto, turn left into the entrance to the distillery. Since Maker's Mark is a National Landmark, there are numerous brown landmark signs along the highways to keep up your spirits. The distillery is closed on major holidays. Tours are usually offered Monday through Saturday, from 10:30 to 3:30. There is a delightful souvenir shop that deserves your attention, managed by Donna Nally, wife of the current master distiller. Although Loretto is a bit out of the way, a visit is well worth the time and trouble.

Seagram

South of Lawrenceburg, down Bond's Mill Road, one can find the Seagram's Bourbon distillery. For years now the Bourbon made here has been virtually unobtainable in the United States. And so while Seagram's Four Roses Bourbons are quite popular abroad (Seagram's claims to be the leading Bourbon in Europe and the third largest brand in the Far East), hardly anybody in the U.S., even in Kentucky, *even* around Lawrenceburg, seems to know that Seagram's has a distillery and makes Bourbon here. This state of affairs, however, is about to change dramatically.

Distilling at this location goes back to the earliest years of Kentucky whiskey-making. In 1818 'Old Joe' Peyton, an Irish immigrant, came from Harrisburg, Pennsylvania, over the mountains and down the river. Legend has it that he came by canoe; but legend also has it that he immediately set up his distillery. Either it was a very large canoe or else a very small still! In any event, he arrived by water to the mouth of Gilbert's Creek, off the Salt River. Finding a suitable limestone spring, he built a still house made of logs and erected a two-bushel-per-day operation.

Using a primitive apparatus by present-day standards, Peyton managed to achieve a reputation for a high-quality product. Quite soon 'Old Joe' became, as far as we know, the first 'brand' whiskey in Kentucky.

Stone foundations for Peyton's 'Old Joe' distillery, though in disrepair, can still be found just a couple of minutes from the present-day Seagram's facility. Deep in some woods, low, decayed stone walls marking the foundations and walls of Peyton's distillery hug Gilbert's Creek. The location was clearly chosen with access in mind, for the water would have provided transportation for supplies and deliveries. Trees now grow where once the mash tub and still would have been. As we wandered around on a warm summer day, guided by Al

The remnants of the original Old Joe Peyton distillery

Mark Waymack

Young from Seagram's, we met a snake or two who seemed to resent our trespassing into history.

In 1840, Old Joe was bought by Gratz Hawkins. In the years that followed, the distillery passed through a dizzying number of hands—Granville Bourbon Hawkins, Medley Bond, T.B. Ripy, Wiley Searcy, and then back to the Hawkins family again. It was the Hawkins family who revived the facility after the repeal of Prohibition, once again using 'Old Joe' as its name. After several more changes of hand, the distillery was acquired by Seagram's in 1943.

The present facility is located on Bond's Mill Road. Advantages over the original Old Joe location included the presence of a mill just across the river as well as a large farm, Wakefield Plantation, close at hand. This meant an easy source of grist without transpor-

The Spanish-style architecture of the Seagram Distillery

tation costs or the expense of having a grain mill within the distillery itself. The present buildings were built in 1910–12 and stand as an unusual, and no doubt the finest, example of Spanish architecture in all of Kentucky.

Some time after Prohibition and until it was purchased by Seagram's, the distillery was owned by the Frankfort Distiller's Corporation. Originating in Atlanta as Paul Jones and Company, but based in Louisville by the end of the century, it was the Frankfort Distiller's Corporation that brought the brand name 'Four Roses' to this distillery's Bourbon, abandoning the Old Joe brand name.

How this brand name was created has sparked numerous different stories. One version involves a Colonel Rose in the 1880s. One day he had been checking his whiskey in the warehouse and thought that the quality of what he had found that day was better than usual. It just so happened that on that particular evening there was a dance in his home. Now, Colonel Rose had four daughters, and on that particular night all four daughters were dressed in black dresses, the height of fashion at the time. They stood on the grand stairway coming down. His wife looked at him and said that since the girls looked so pretty that evening, shouldn't they have a corsage or something? So Colonel Rose went out into the garden and cut four roses and gave one to each of the girls. While he thought his girls looked quite fetching, he also knew their temperament. His wife then suggested, "Maybe that's a name you could use for the Bourbon you've been talking about—Call it 'Four Roses'? It's such a mellow idea." Colonel Rose thought this was particularly appropriate, for, as he said, "I like to think of Four Roses as mellow, but certainly not tame."

Like so many good stories, this one is disputable. A descendant of the Rose family in Atlanta has retorted that there were five, not four, Roses in the family of Rufus Rose. Furthermore, the men were gentlemen, and would certainly not have dragged their Southern ladies into the publicizing of whiskey. She then concludes that the name came from the four male Roses—her uncle, her father, and their two sons. Another story suggests that the name arose from the

Al Young checking the mash at Seagram's

Mark Waymack

fact that Rufus Rose held four retail establishments. Other stories abound, including one that claims the Rose family had nothing to do with naming Four Roses; instead the brand name appeared much later from some quite different source.

Whatever the real story, the Seagram's plant, under the direction of its master distiller, Ova Haney, is quite busy producing Bourbon. Production now stands at around 9,500 proof gallons per day.

Water comes either from underground limestone springs or from the adjacent Salt River, which is fed by rich limestone springs. The mash is reputed to be slow and gentle.

Four Roses uses 20 fermenters. Seven of these are modern stainless steel, while 13 are cypress tanks. In bygone years Seagram's owned and operated several distilleries in the area. As these were closed in a process of consolidation, all of the old cypress tanks were dismantled and transported to the current location. There they were reconstructed, and there they are treated to this day with tender loving care.

Traditional Bourbon warehouses stand on the ground surrounding the distillery. However, Four Roses Bourbon is not aged in these warehouses: they are leased to Wild Turkey. Instead, after the spirit

One of the cypress fermenting tanks still in use at Seagrams

Mark Waymack

comes of the still, it is pumped into tank trucks. These trucks then drive 50 miles down the road to the Cox's Creek location. This spot was, in the heyday of Seagram's Bourbon distilling, at the center of its many distillery plants.

Here at Cox's Creek, the tanks are pumped into a cistern, then into the barrels. Unlike all other Bourbon, Seagram's Four Roses is aged in one-storey buildings, more akin to Scottish warehouses than traditional Bourbon warehouses. Ova Haney argues that the one-story warehouse provides ideal aging conditions. The great variances in climate between the top of a nine-storey warehouse and the ground level can be remarkable. Other distillers have dealt with this either by laboriously rotating their stock or, more simply, marrying barrels from a variety of warehouse locations to produce an overall desirable product. By using one-storey warehousing, Four Roses obviates all of those problems.

Finally, reflecting its Scottish connections and its European market, Four Roses Bourbon, when it is properly matured, is pumped from the barrels at Cox's Creek into stainless steel containers, from whence it is trucked to the seaboard and shipped to Scotland where it is bottled at a Seagram's facility. From there it is shipped primarily to Europe and Asia. Indeed, when we visited the Four Roses Distillery, there was no aged Bourbon to be had for a tasting! Anything bottled was outside the country, and anything suitably aged in a barrel was 50 miles away at Cox's Creek.

Since the first printing of this book two dramatic changes have taken place at Seagram's. First, Ova Haney has retired, being given the title of Master Distiller Emeritus. Jim Rutledge, a long-time Seagram's employee, is now at the helm at the Four Roses Distillery. Second, Seagram's will introduce a Bourbon to the U. S. market in January 1996—*Four Roses Single Barrel Reserve*. At first it will be limited in distribution to Kentucky and Indiana, but national distribution is the eventual plan,

We have finally had the pleasure of tasting Four Roses. Our first sample came to us by way of a hotel room in Xian, China. Later we were fortunate to taste a sample of the Four Roses Single Barrel Reserve, which, we are happy to say, is a delightful Bourbon.

TASTING NOTES

Four Roses Single Barrel Reserve, 43 percent

This whiskey has a wonderful, deep amber color. The nose is warm and rich, with round malty tones. On the palate it is drier than most Bourbons, emphasizing the small grains, full in body and flavor without being at all heavy. Indeed, it leans a bit in the direction of a malt Scotch whisky rather than that of the sweeter Bourbons. The finish is long, warm, and quite smooth. A bit unusual by common Bourbon standards, we found this to be a well-crafted, highly enjoyable whiskey.

VISITING

While Seagram's Four Roses does not have anything like a visitor center or scheduled tours, they will hospitably entertain guests with suitable advance notice. Even if you don't get to taste the Bourbon, the unusual architecture is by itself worth a visit.

South of Lawrenceburg, the plant is at 1224 Bond's Mill Road, west of Route 62, just a stone's throw north of the Bluegrass Parkway. Do call ahead. The telephone number is 502-839-3436.

United Distillers

To write a short but adequate account of United Distillers and their role in the saga of American whiskey is a daunting if not impossible task. The story could be told either in a very short and not very satisfactory fashion, or in a very long and convoluted manner.

The problem is this: While United Distillers is a relative newcomer to the American whiskey business, it has gotten into the trade by acquiring several old distilleries, each with long and complex histories of their own.

The 1970s and 1980s were not easy times for the Bourbon industry. Production had been quite high, anticipating increasing demand for Bourbon whiskeys. Unfortunately, there was a consumer move towards 'lighter' spirits, such as gin and vodka, and also away from spirits towards wine. Hence, many distilleries became financially over-extended and foundered.

Just as they had bought up an incredibly large share of the Scotch whisky industry, United Distillers decided that this down cycle offered a good chance to acquire a presence in the American whiskey market. This would be useful, not only in terms of having hopefully profitable Bourbon distilleries in its portfolio; it might also help to gain access to the American market for the corporation's Scotch whiskies.

The process of consolidation in the Bourbon industry is amply evident in the threads that lead to United Distillers' current position. Glenmore Distilleries bought both Medley Distilling Company and Fleischmann Distilling Company before United Distillers bought Glenmore, thus inheriting Medley and Fleischmann. Schenley Distillers had acquired Bernheim as well as George Dickel (the Cascade Distillery of Tennessee) prior to its acquisition by United Distillers. And finally, United Distillers also purchased the Stitzel-Weller, who had acquired Old Fitzgerald. Thus, seven distinct distilleries have been brought together into the United Distillers' fold.

Several of these facilities were in mothballs when they were acquired; several more were shuttered after their acquisition by United Distillers. These distilleries often came with Bourbon in their warehouses. They also typically came with colorful histories and long lists of brand labels. For example, when United acquired Bernheim, Bernheim alone held the rights to more than 90 different labels.

Sensitive to its new-found history, United Distillers has created a 'heritage' department, with at least two full-time archivists/historians. These fellows—Chris Morris and Michael Veach when we visited—have *years* of work ahead of them. The historical records gathered from these various acquired concerns easily pack several rooms. And bringing some sense of order to the materials, including such basic things as a cataloging system, will be arduous tasks.

The corporation knew very well why these distilleries were on the market, and it has been in the process of consolidation from the very beginning of its presence in Kentucky. The Fleischmann plants are all closed. Medley Distilling, in Owensboro, is now strictly a warehousing operation. Glenmore, also in Owensboro, is used for both warehousing and bottling. Active distilling has been confined to two facilities—the Bernheim Distillery and the Stitzel-Weller Distillery—both in Louisville.

Not only has United Distillers been consolidating its production activity; it is also consolidating its active brands. While United Distillers may well hold one of the largest catalogues of brand names and labels, it constrains its activity to five key Bourbon brands. Those brands are: I.W. Harper; Old Charter; Old Fitzgerald; Rebel Yell; and W.L. Weller Special Reserve.

Unlike Scotch, Bourbon is an *American* product. And it is also true that Bourbon has been made essentially by *Americans*. Now the famous Scotch whisky distilleries, in their farflung locations, tend to be quite rooted. When a Scottish distiller is faced with insufficient capacity, his first (and probably only) thought is how to expand the capacity at his present location. But the American business spirit is remarkably different. When an American distiller is faced with inadequate capacity, his first thought has usually been, 'To whom can I sell my current plant so that I can take my capital and build a newer, more efficient, bigger one elsewhere?' Consequently, very few distilling companies, and very few labels, are in their original locations.

For example, one of the two United Distillers' distilleries is the Stitzel-Weller plant. The Stitzel brothers, Frederick and Philip, started in 1870 with a small distillery at 26th and Broadway in Louisville, which soon burned and was rebuilt. Feeling themselves confined, they built yet another new distillery not too far away which was used until 1935. Then, Stitzel and Weller merged, and built a whole new distillery, the one that is currently in use.

The second United Distillers' plant, the Bernheim, shares a similar history. The Bernheim site has a history of distilling going back at least to the 1880s, but the Bernheims were not the first ones there.

Isaac W. Bernheim, according to his autobiography, began his career in America as a peddler in Pennsylvania. The quick success of this enterprise inspired him to purchase his own horse and cart to increase his opportunities in the business. Winter came, and he stabled his new horse with a friend for the coldest months. But that spring, when he went to collect his horse and resume using the horse-drawn cart, his friend informed him that the horse had died. Bernheim couldn't afford yet another horse, so he sold off all his inventory and went to work for an uncle who lived in Paducah, Kentucky. The year was 1872.

In Paducah, he fell in love with Bourbon—not just as a drink, but also as a business possibility. So he had his brother, Bernard, come down and join him. They bought a barrel of whiskey and set up a business.

Finally, in 1903, Isaac Bernheim, Bernard Bernheim (who patented the hip flask in 1900), and Isaac's son, Leon Bernheim, incorporated and built their first manufacturing plant. Canny businessmen, during their reign over the corporation, Bernheim Distilling eventually held 97 different labels. Apparently the last of the Bernheims, Isaac, retired from the business in 1915 and died in 1945.

Curiously, the flagship whiskey of the Bernheims was I.W. Harper. Perhaps the Bernheims felt that the American public wasn't quite ready for a good ole southern Bourbon with a Jewish name on it.

According to a letter from Bernheim, brought to our attention by Michael Veach, I.W. Bernheim developed a friendship with a horse-racing man named Harper. This Harper managed to own horses that ran in the first two Kentucky Derbys. So, the 'I.W.' come from Bernheim's first two initials, and the "Harper" is in honor of his race-horse-owning friend.

One other character that deserves mention is Frederick Stitzel. Though not well remembered, Stitzel was the individual who invented and patented (in 1879) the 'open-rick' warehousing system that is used, to this day, by virtually every whiskey distillery in the U.S.

Old Fitzgerald, the whiskey, is named for John E. Fitzgerald, who founded the distillery in 1870, and named it after himself. The Old Fitzgerald Distillery was originally located, however, in Frankfort, not Louisville. The brand moved to Louisville when the Stitzel Distillery (founded by the brothers Philip and Frederick Stitzel) merged with the company of William Larue Weller, and the new Stitzel-Weller Distillery opened on Kentucky Derby Day in 1935.

United Distillers is trying to draw this tangled skein of history together into five meaningful brands. This is accomplished by using two different plants, two different grain formulas, a variety of process differences (such as the proof of the distillate as it comes off the still), as well as aging differences. The result is that there are five distinct Bourbon brands that fall into two different family groupings.

One family is the Bernheim family, which are all distilled at the Bernheim plant: I.W. Harper and Old Charter. The actual Bernheim plant is a relative newcomer, having been rebuilt a few years ago at a cost of around ten million dollars, incorporating the latest in Bourbon-making technology.

The Bernheim family of Bourbons all share the same basic grain formula. It is high in rye, low in corn. This makes for a fairly full body, with a characteristic rye 'bite.'

As it acquired distillery after distillery, United Distillers had the opportunity to collect together a number of cypress fermenting tanks. Nevertheless, they have chosen to go strictly with stainless steel fermenters, for the sake of *quality*. The old cypress tanks are very difficult to keep clean. With each fermentation, various bacteria and wild yeasts try their best to get a foothold. A complete sterilization prevents these micro-organisms from having the chance to develop enough in population size to have any influence on the taste characteristics of the whiskey. But if sufficient numbers of such microbes remain viable, lurking in the fermenter, then they have a kind of head start with the next batch. Enough of them, and the organoleptic qualities of the whiskey can be adversely affected. One of the most easily identifiable effects of such contamination is the presence of 'butterscotch' tones in the whiskey. United Distillers, therefore, prefers to go with stainless steel, a material that is easy to sterilize.

The Bernheim still is a copper and stainless steel still, manufactured by Vendome. The Stitzel-Weller still, also by Vendome, is in the purists' tradition, being made by Vendome of 100 percent copper.

The beer still, with covers off to show the inside, at the Old Fitzgerald plant

Mark Waymack

Like Wild Turkey and Maker's Mark, United Distillers claims to have the lowest proof off the still and into the barrel. Lacking any hard figures, however, this claim is difficult to ascertain. From the final products, it would seem safe to conclude that the Bernheim whiskeys *do* come off the still at low proofs and do go into the barrel at relatively low proofs. There is a price to pay for this preference. One way of producing a 'cleaner' whiskey is to distill at a higher proof, since doing so leaves more of the congeners behind in the spent beer rather than carrying them through into the distilled spirit. This, however, produces a very bland-tasting whiskey. The gains to be had from a low proof from the still are in the form of more flavor components, consequently a richer-tasting whiskey. If you are going to come off the still at a low proof, and have a whiskey that is *both* clean and full-flavored, you will have to have a 'cleaner' mash (far less bacterial and wild yeast infection).

With regard to aging, it is more economical to age at a higher proof. If the whiskey goes into the barrel at 125 proof, then the same amount of alcohol fits into fewer barrels. Fewer barrels means lower costs in purchasing and lower costs in warehouse space. When the aging is done, the whiskey is cut with more water to bring it to appropriate bottling proof.

Aging in the barrel at a lower proof, however, means that the effects of the barrel are less diluted when the whiskey finally goes into the bottle. Hence, a Bourbon that goes into the barrel at 110 proof, and ages the same time as one that goes in at 125 proof, will wind up with richer barrel tones when bottled at the same final proof. So, if you want to produce a whiskey that emphasizes the wood, caramel, and vanilla—characteristics of Bourbon—then using a lower barrel proof is one way of getting there. United Distillers has chosen to use low barrel proofs at both its Bernheim and Stitzel-Weller operations. Finally, the Bernheim whiskeys tend to be aged far longer than the industry norm.

The Stitzel-Weller family of Bourbons includes: Old Fitzgerald, Rebel Yell, and Weller. A signpost outside the mature-looking, Georgian-style brick building proudly declares, "No Chemists Allowed." We seriously doubt that this imperative is strictly obeyed; but it

The posted philosophy of Old Fitzgerald— "No chemists allowed"

James Harris

does reveal something about the Stitzel-Weller philosophy of Bourbon-making—it is an *art* more than a *science*.

The Stitzel-Weller family all share a wheat formula. Maker's Mark gets a great deal of marketing mileage out of its use of wheat in place of rye. In fact, Old Fitzgerald has for long been a wheat-rather-than-rye whiskey. Indeed, the Stitzel-Weller folks are credited with sharing their formula and yeast with T.W. Samuels, Sr., when he bought the Happy Hollow Distillery in Loretto and turned it into Maker's Mark.

In the hands of the Stitzel-Weller crew, the wheat recipe produces a Bourbon that is 'soft,' as contrasted with rye formulas. But these whiskeys are also 'big' whiskeys, seeming to be perhaps more full-bodied and a little sharper or more robust around the edges, so to speak, than Maker's Mark.

Once again, all of the Stitzel-Weller Bourbons (Old Fitzgerald, W.L. Weller, Rebel Yell) are supposed to come off the still at a low proof and into the barrel at a low proof. They are certainly aged far longer than the industry norm. Some of the Stitzel-Weller products

Rolling barrels from the warehouse to go to bottling

Mark Waymack

are bottled at ten, twelve, even 14 years of age. And while most Bourbons seem to peak at seven to nine years (at least by our taste), the Stitzel-Weller whiskeys seem to mature gracefully, without becoming woody or losing their integrity.

TASTING NOTES

Old Charter, 43 percent, 10-year

A very mellow whiskey. The aroma is subtle, even a bit light. In the mouth, the whiskey has a touch of char and subtle vanilla tones. The long aging has smoothed out any rough edges.

I.W. Harper, 40 percent

This is clearly younger than its sibling, Old Charter. There are strong, fresh barrel tones—wood and char—in the aroma. In the mouth it is a big whiskey, full of character. The taste has a sweet streak, with perhaps some apple hints. There is a noticeable rye edge, though we would not call it bitter. Finally, there is a long, warm finish.

Old Fitzgerald, 50 percent

Old Fitz comes in several different proofs and ages. We sampled the 100 proof version. This is a big whiskey. The wheat, instead of rye, contributes to a definite softness. It is deep, round and very warm in the mouth. There is an incredibly long finish, with hints of spice. An excellent whiskey, and at a bargain price as well.

W.L. Weller, 45 percent

Once again, the wheat makes for a soft whiskey. This is very round on the palate, with touches of vanilla-caramel sweetness. Though it is deep, it manages somehow to be a tad lighter than (and not quite as complex as) Old Fitz.

Rebel Yell, 40 percent

A somewhat unusual, fairly distinctive whiskey. Since it comes from Stitzel-Weller, it shares the wheat formula of Old Fitz. At the same time, it has more of an aggressive edge to it. At least in the bottle we sampled, those aggressive edges overpowered the soft, wheat middle—like a Dixieland jazz band made up of some brash brass and mellow clarinets, but without any of the reedy saxophone.

VISITING

United Distillers is not equipped to handle visitors at its Louisville facilities; but it does host guests at its George Dickel Distillery in Tullahoma, Tennessee. (See the next chapter for information on Dickel.)

Wild Turkey

High atop some bluffs, above the Kentucky River, stands the Boulevard Distilling Company, previously known as Austin Nichols Distilling, but more commonly recognized by its famous products—Wild Turkey, Rare Breed, and more recently Kentucky Spirit, all classic Kentucky Bourbons.

Distilling in this general area, outside of Lawrenceburg, goes back to the early 1800s. Indeed, prior to Prohibition, one could see six different distilleries from where Boulevard Distilling now stands.

Corporate headquarters, under the banner of Austin Nichols (a subsidiary of Pernod-Ricard, who also control two notable Scotch whisky distilleries: Abelour and Edradour), are in New York. But that seems quite far away, and when we visited it was clearly Jimmy Russell who was in charge.

The distillery buildings date back to 1905, when the three Ripy brothers, E.F. Ripy, J.C. Ripy, and Forest Ripy, incorporated and built their new distillery with a capacity of 162 bushels per day, probably about 15 barrels per day. The brand name was, not surprisingly, 'Ripy Bros.'

Revived after Prohibition, the distillery seems to have operated under the Ripy name until 1971, when Austin Nichols bought it and identified it as the Wild Turkey Distillery. Since then, all Wild Turkey Bourbon has been produced at this Lawrenceburg facility. The Wild Turkey brand itself dates back to shortly after Prohibition was repealed. As Jimmy Russell recounted the story, it had nothing to do with wild turkeys around the distillery (though there are reputed to be quite a few). In fact, it had nothing to do with wild turkeys in Kentucky, but goes back to a McCarthy family tradition.

"To the best of my knowledge," Russell related, "the McCarthy family, up in New York, started the Wild Turkey brand. Old man McCarthy and a bunch of his friends had a wild turkey hunt each

Mark Waymack

The Wild Turkey distillery

year down in the Carolinas. As they went on the turkey hunt, they'd each bring a part of the provisions.

"McCarthy brought the Bourbon one year, out of his warehouse. And the men all started talking about the Bourbon, how good it tasted, some of the best Bourbon they'd ever had.

"Well, the next year, when it was time to go on the turkey hunt again, they called up McCarthy and told him to bring some more of the Bourbon he had brought last year.

"Now, really, he didn't remember exactly what he'd brought, but with all the government records he had to keep, he could go back and figure out what he had brought. Turns out it was some eight year old, 101 proof.

"So, he took the same kind of stuff—eight-year-old, 101 proof — and they all liked it immensely again. So, being a canny business-man, he decided to market it, and he called it 'Wild Turkey.'"

The combination of an engaging label backed up by a skillful distiller has worked well for Wild Turkey, for the plant has grown steadily from the 162-bushel-a-day operation under the Ripy brothers to 2,500 bushels per day. In fact, since coming to this distillery, Wild Turkey has never had a year of decreased sales!

As we started our tour through the distillery, Jimmy Russell warned us that we're "not going to see a showcase here, just an old-fashioned distillery. I've been around a long time, and I'm a little old fashioned about making Bourbon whiskey." Having gotten into the art of distilling in the early 1950s, and having been at it steadily since then, Jimmy Russell no doubt deserves the right to run the distillery the ways he thinks best.

The first example of being 'old-fashioned' is the operating season. Out of principle, not necessity, Russell insists that the plant shut down production during July and August. In his opinion, it's just too hot either to operate the still properly or to put it in the barrel properly.

A second example of old-fashionedness at Wild Turkey is the formula. Wild Turkey's formula is somewhat different from that of most other Bourbon distilleries. Whereas quite a few distilleries proudly emphasize the high percentage of corn in their mash (pointing out that it helps make a lighter whiskey), Wild Turkey goes in the opposite direction—using less corn, and hence far more malt and rye than others. The result is a fuller, richer, denser whiskey.

Russell compares making the Bourbon mash to cooking a soup. A really good soup contains a variety of ingredients. But as any good cook knows, not all of those ingredients require the same cooking times or temperatures. Diced potatoes, when added along with the beef or onions or carrots at the beginning of the soup-making, will be nothing but mush when the other ingredients are finally done. So, each ingredient must be added at the appropriate stage in the cooking process.

The corn first cooks in the water for a couple of hours by itself. Then, the temperature is allowed to fall to less than 170 degrees Fahrenheit, at which point the rye is introduced. As Russell explains, "If you cook the rye at too high a temperature you cook its bitterness into the mash." Finally, as the temperature drops into the low 150s, the malt is introduced and the 'mashing' begins.

Temperature is a critical aspect of an effective mash. The temperature must be tightly maintained between 148 and 152 degrees Fahrenheit, so that the enzymes in the malted barley work effec-

Fermenting mash in the cypress tanks at Wild Turkey.

Mark Waymack

tively. Too high a temperature, and they are destroyed; too low a temperature and the enzymes won't work at a reasonable rate. A second important factor is acidity. And when working with limestone-rich water, which is alkaline, this can be a problem. Diastase, the enzyme, isn't too keen on alkaline environments, so at Wild Turkey some of the acidic backset, also known less nobly as 'thin slop,' is mixed into the mash to increase its acidity and boost the activity of the enzymes.

After the mash is completed, it is pumped into the fermenters, along with the usual portion of backset by which a whiskey is called sour mash.

Wild Turkey uses a 'sour' yeast. What this means is that unlike many distilleries which maintain their yeast cultures in a 'sweet' growth medium of maltose, Wild Turkey maintains its yeast in a 'sour' culture medium. Russell uses some of the thin slop for this purpose. The alcohol has been taken out in the distillation process, but as a natural effect of the yeast activity, the thin slop is, as noted before, somewhat acidic. To prevent any bacterial contamination, this liquid is boiled. It is then used to mash some malted barley. The resulting liquid is sweet in the sense that it has the maltose that the yeast needs to propagate, but it is also sour in the sense that it is acidic.

The Wild Turkey philosophy would seem to be that if you want a yeast that will be vigorous in the acidic environment of a sour mash fermentation, you ought to culture it in a suitably sour environment. What grows well in the acidic dona will ferment well in the acidic sour mash.

The Vendome column still reeks of tradition. It is strictly a copper affair, for Russell refuses to have anything to do with stainless steel. Whatever the chemical reactions are, the stainless columns, even when scrap copper is liberally thrown in on top of the plates in the column, just don't give the right result, according to Russell.

Then, Russell insists, the white dog comes off the beer still and the doubler at much lower proofs than the industry average—yielding a richer, more full-bodied spirit than most. Furthermore, the spirit goes into the barrel at a far lower proof than most other Bourbons. Trade secrets are just that, secret, and Russell is tight-lipped about exact percentages and exact proofs. But in a way, the truth is already out, for Wild Turkey's 'Rare Breed' is advertised as being bottled at "barrel proof." And the neck label on each bottles identifies the proof of that batch. The range seems to be from about 109.6 to 112.2 proof. (Note as a point of comparison that barrel proof for Jim Beam's small-batch Booker's Bourbon runs around 125 proof.)

We can safely conclude that the spirit goes into the barrel at something less than 55 percent—and that is certainly far lower than the norm for the industry, vying with Maker's Mark for the right to be called the lowest in the business. This makes for a far richer, fuller-flavored product than most other Bourbons.

As we approached the warehouses, Russell once again took the opportunity to emphasize the 'natural way' that characterizes making Wild Turkey. As he said, "I just feel, see, everything about Wild Turkey is a natural process. Our storage buildings are natural. The outside temperature controls the aging process. We have no artifi-

Jimmy Russell checking the new spirit as it flows through the tailbox

Mark Waymack

cial heat. We open the windows in the summertime to get the good air circulating, and close them in the winter. We just feel you do a better job of the aging process in that way."

Furthermore, Wild Turkey insists upon keeping with the labor-intensive practice of rotating barrels—starting them on the top floors and working them down to the bottom. And like all responsible distillers, Russell and his team monitor the resting barrels, making the periodic taste check.

By the sixth year, approximately 30 percent of the barrel's volume has been lost to evaporation. By the eighth year it is 33 percent and by the twelfth year, the Angel's Share is about 40 percent. But, as Mr. Russell reiterates, if a third hasn't evaporated, it's not ready yet. "If a third isn't gone, the Angel hasn't gotten his share, so it's not any good yet."

It's hard to find room to argue with a man like Jimmy Russell. Under his direction, the plant now produces some 60,000–65,000 barrels per year, and demand for Wild Turkey and Rare Breed continues to rise.

Rare Breed, introduced in 1991, is made by combining select barrels of Wild Turkey six-year-old, eight-year-old, and twelve-year-old. This is then bottled at barrel proof, a range between 109.6 and 112.2 proof. When asked why or how that formula was decided upon, Jimmy Russell's ready response is, "Because that's what we like." What else would you expect from a man who clearly knows his craft?

In the Fall of 1994 Wild Turkey introduced a single-barrel Bourbon, Kentucky Spirit. As Russell explains, "What I'm doing in the single-barrel version is tasting each single barrel to keep that special quality and consistency." Not surprisingly, barrels for Kentucky Spirit tend to come from the heart of the warehouses, where climate fluctuations are muted. And what Russell is looking for is "that deep amber color, that good vanilla-caramel flavor along with a touch of sweetness."

A special processing area has been set aside with a one-barrel dumping trough, a one-barrel filter, and a small, largely manual bottling line.

Kentucky Spirit is bottled at that classic Wild Turkey strength: 101 proof.

For international travellers, Wild Turkey will also be available as a single-barrel version bottled at barrel proof and called Kentucky Legend. If you're not a jet-setter yourself, try to find someone you can somehow bribe into bringing a bottle back for you!

TASTING NOTES

Wild Turkey 101, 50.5 percent

This is a big, deep whiskey. The color is a beautiful amber. The nose is rich—mellow, a hint of sweetness. On the palate it is big: a full-bodied Bourbon, full of character. The high percentage of small grains is quite evident in the slightly dry, heavy, malty, toffee-like tones. The low proof off the still and into the barrel translate into an exceedingly deep Bourbon. The finish is longer, lingering and pleasant. Do not waste this by mixing it with anything else!

Wild Turkey 101, 50.5 percent, twelve-year

The nose is quite nice: reasonably rich, with some slight flowery notes. On the palate this is a rich whiskey, and the high malt and rye content show. Malty, some caramel, and with just a touch of vanilla. It has a *long,* warm finish.

Wild Turkey, 40 percent, no age specified

While this is a less intense drink than the "101" version, it still exhibits the full-bodied, "old-fashioned" style that Jimmy Russell affirms.

Rare Breed, (55 percent in our sample, but variable), mixture of six-, eight-, and 12-year

Quite similar to Wild Turkey 101. The higher proof makes for a more intense drink, concentrating the Wild Turkey flavors into what should only be a true 'sippin' whiskey.' The melding of different years yields more complexity. The six-year probably adds a certain freshness, a lively bite. The twelve-year introduces deeper toffee or caramel tones and a little more wood. Bourbon doesn't get much better than this.

Kentucky Spirit—Single-Barrel, 50.5 percent

The packaging on this alone should receive some sort of award. The decanter-like shape is quite graceful. (After savoring a few shots of Kentucky Spirit, an over-active imagination might even see the bottle shape as a highly stylized version of a wild turkey viewed from the front.) The wild turkey icon is present as an image stamped in the over-sized metal cap that holds the cork. But packaging aside, this is a splendid Bourbon. It shares many characteristics of its sibling, Wild Turkey 101. The color is a deep amber. The aroma is rich: rounded, full, balanced. On the palate, the small grains show in the relatively dry, malty, full-bodied taste. There are caramel-vanilla notes, with a touch of sweetness; but this should not be thought of as a sweet Bourbon. Mellow is a well-deserved adjective.

VISITING

Boulevard Distilling, the home of Wild Turkey, is an easy drive from Lexington. Located on the edge of the Kentucky River, on the outskirts of Lawrenceburg, it is accessible where Route 62 crosses the river. Going east from Lawrenceburg, take Route 62 for 2.3 miles. Then turn right on Route 1510.

The distillery offers tours. It is open to visitors Monday through Friday from 9:00 A.M. to 4:00 P.M. Tours are at 9:00, 10:30, 12:30, and 2:30. Advance notice is appreciated for large groups. (Telephone 502-839-4544) There is a charming souvenir and gift shop on the premises.

4

Tennessee

Although Tennessee is usually identified as a 'deep-south' state, it is, in many ways, a border state separating not only North from South but East from West—and also old from new. The state is over 400 miles long—east to west—and spans the land from the Appalachian Mountains to the Mississippi River. The mountains in the eastern part of the state proved a formidable obstacle for early settlers. In fact, the earliest explorations of what is now Tennessee by Europeans took place from the south and the west. The Spanish explorer De Soto explored the southern part of Tennessee in 1540 and made his way to the Mississippi River, near what is now Memphis. French explorers came down the Mississippi River from the Great Lakes region and into Tennessee from the West. La Salle is said to have reached the bluffs on the Mississippi River, near Memphis, in 1682. The French, however, did not attempt to colonize the area since they were only interested in trading with the Indians. The name "Tennessee" is supposedly derived from "Tanasie," the name of one of the largest Cherokee settlements in the area when the white, European settlers arrived.

Colonization did slowly come from the east along the Wilderness Trail, blazed by Daniel Boone, and down the Cumberland River from Kentucky. It was, for the most part, the same Scotch-Irish who had moved from Virginia and Pennsylvania into Kentucky, and they brought with them their small, copper potstills and their knowledge of distilling—just as they did in Kentucky.

These settlers found rich farm land with extended growing seasons and mild winters. The mountains and rolling piedmont in the eastern part of the state made for many small farms—a departure from the huge plantations of the coastal plains of Virginia and North Carolina. Making whiskey was as much a part of the normal routine among the early white settlers in Tennessee as were making bread or bacon. Nothing went to waste on the frontier, and whatever corn meal was available after making other things was made into whiskey, which, of course, would keep indefinitely without refrigeration.

The many rivers which can be found through the state flow north, south and west and opened the territory beyond in the early days of the American frontier. In fact, it is said that anywhere in Tennessee, you are never further than 20 miles from a river with navigable water. Many early settlers who made their ways south into Alabama and Mississippi and west into Arkansas and beyond did so because of the inviting river travel through Tennessee.

These same rivers carried whiskey to the south and the west. The rivers were the main conduit for commerce. As early as the turn of the nineteenth century, whiskey made in Tennessee was being shipped by flatbottom river boats down the Mississippi River to New Orleans. Tennessee thus used its central locality and its river access to neighboring areas to spread both its people and its products—including its whiskey—to the rest of its country. Even today, no other state borders more than eight states, as Tennessee does.

A Sense of Place

Perhaps the same is said about people from other states, but since its earliest beginnings, Tennessee has been known to produce people with a keen 'sense of place.' In today's mobile society where people frequently move several times during a lifetime—from state to state or across the country—feeling a strong attachment to a particular

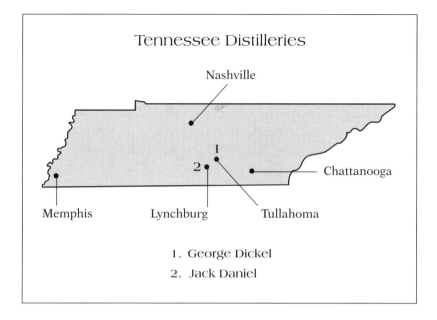

Tennessee Distilleries

Nashville

1

2

Chattanooga

Memphis   Lynchburg   Tullahoma

1. George Dickel
2. Jack Daniel

state or region has become somewhat unusual or even quaint. For most Tennesseans, such an attachment to a locality is part of their nature. Tennesseans usually identify themselves as being from a particular region of the state—east Tennessee (the mountains), middle Tennessee (the rolling hills of the Piedmont), or west Tennessee (the wide, flat plains of the Mississippi Delta). There is a great friendly rivalry among Tennesseans from different areas of the state. As a young child, Harris, a native Tennessean, remembers his father, a native of Tullahoma and thus a middle Tennessean, telling how the people in east Tennessee had to breed a special breed of cattle to live on the sides of the mountains with two legs on one side shorter than the two on the other side. It was several years before the gullible Harris realized that it was his leg which was being pulled.

Another favorite story about Tennesseans involves the newcomer to Heaven who arrives at the Pearly Gates and is then taken on an introductory tour by St. Peter. Everywhere the newcomer goes he sees people experiencing the expected eternal bliss and happiness in the ethereal perfection of Heaven. Finally, they come to a group of people who are chained to trees, and the newcomer asks St. Peter what is going on. "Well," St. Peter explains, "these are Tennesseans. They're supposed to be here, but we have to keep them chained up to keep them from trying to go back to Tennessee!" Such long-standing stories about Tennessee might well have prompted the familiar line from a well-known country song, "If Heaven ain't a lot like Dixie, I don't wanta go there." The many small farms of early Tennessee also produced a brand of Tennessean with a fiery independence. The nickname of the state, "the Volunteer State," captures well the fierce independence of Tennesseans. Very early, Tennesseans showed the disposition to handle their own problems on their own and independently of the eastern colonies. The Watauga Association, former in 1772, was the first attempt to bring law and order to the Tennessee frontier by means of a democratic constitution. This was followed, in 1779, by the Cumberland Contract which provided for a similar democratic, representative government for settlers along the Cumberland River near Nashboro (Nashville).

Tennessee Volunteers

The first Tennessee Volunteers, though not members of the regular Continental Army, showed their independence as well as their courage, by marching all the way from Eastern Tennessee across the Smoky Mountains to Kings Mountain, South Carolina, to fight the Battle of Kings Mountain against the British in 1780. But even this was a personal quarrel with the British who had threatened to cross the mountains into Tennessee and attack the area included in the Watauga Association. The volunteers went to war to defend their homes and Tennessee rather than fighting for the independence of the colonies. They won the battle, then packed up and went home, and left behind stories about the "boys from Tennessee" and, of course, the whiskey which they had carried with them. When they got home, they promptly formed their own state, the State of Franklin, and seceded from the State of North Carolina in 1784. As we have seen earlier, only a master stroke of diplomacy, which eventually resulted in Tennessee becoming the sixteenth state in 1796, resolved the embarrassing situation for the United States government.

Tennessee Volunteers earned fame again at the Battle of New Orleans in 1814 when they helped Andrew Jackson defeat the British. The fighting men from Tennessee were famous for two things: their marksmanship with the long rifle and their whiskey. Later, capitalizing upon his fame, Jackson was responsible for breaking the stranglehold which the wealthy and aristocratic Virginians had held on the presidency, when he won on a populist ticket in 1828. As a result, Tennessee whiskey made its way into the White House for the first time. James Polk continued the tradition after Jackson. It is illustrative of the strength and character of the young, unsettled frontier state of Tennessee that it could produce two presidents in the infancy of our country. Some historians consider the facts that Tennessee was the last southern state to secede from the Union in 1861, and the first to be readmitted to the Union in 1866 as further indications of the independence of Tennesseans and the role of the state as a border state.

Early Tennesseans

Tennessee is responsible for providing early American history with many of its greatest heroes. We have already seen that Andrew Jackson, 'Old Hickory,' was from Tennessee. Davy Crockett, killed at the Alamo on March 6, 1836, as a 'volunteer,' was a Tennessean and a three-term Congressman from Tennessee. Crockett is immortalized as an independent frontier man, but few people realize that the reason he left Tennessee was that he opposed the forced removal of the Cherokee Indians from the state. The removal of the Cherokee was a volatile issue which pitted Andrew Jackson who supported it against Crockett who opposed it. Crockett voted against the bill in Congress, but it passed anyway. So Crockett left Tennessee and headed for Texas, and the long and deadly forced march of the Cherokee from Tennessee to Oklahoma ensued—what has become known as the 'Trail of Tears.'

Sam Houston, who earned famed by defeating Santa Anna, then becoming the first President of the Republic of Texas, and then the first Governor of the State of Texas, was from Tennessee. Houston may well be unique in American history in having served as a congressman, senator, and governor of one state (Tennessee), then as President of a Republic, and then as governor of a second state (Texas). True to his Tennessee heritage of independence, Houston resigned in protest as Governor of Texas when Texas seceded from the Union in 1861.

The story of the involvement of the people of Tennessee during the Civil War is much too long and involved to be told here. There were more battles fought in Tennessee than in any other state except Virginia, and the men who came to Tennessee to fight—Northerners and Southerners alike—went home with memories and stories about Tennessee and an appetite for the fine, 'Tennessee whiskey' that they found there. The special charcoal mellowing process (which we shall describe in some detail shortly) was a well-established part of the process of making Tennessee whiskey by the time of the Civil War, and it was probably from this time that the description 'Tennessee Whiskey' first came to be widely used as a way of identifying the whiskey made in this manner. It was to take another eighty years for the Internal Revenue Service to officially recognize Tennessee whiskey as a legally distinct *kind* of whiskey.

Tennessee Today

Today, Tennessee is still a border state between the old and the new. The Tennessee Valley Authority and the Oak Ridge Nuclear Laboratory represent two of the most permanent changes brought by the twentieth century, and the same modern technology which is representative of these twentieth-century industries has also found its way into the whiskey industry. However, within the modern Tennessee whiskey industry, important elements of an earlier and simpler time have been preserved. At both Jack Daniel's Old Time Distillery in Cave Spring Hollow and at George Dickel's Distillery in Cascade Hollow a unique way of making whiskey, now over 150 years old, has been maintained. Tennessee Whiskey is made today in much the same manner as it was by the earliest Scotch-Irish settlers. Tennessee Whiskey is a border between the old and the new; it is both old and new at the same time.

Tennessee Whiskey

Now there is still quite a bit of confusion about the exact nature of Tennessee Whiskey. Many bar arguments and wagers are won or lost over exactly what *kind* of whiskey Jack Daniel's or George Dickel really is. Tennessee Whiskey is a unique designation of a special *kind* of whiskey. It is not a Bourbon. It is not a rye. Tennessee Whiskey is a straight whiskey which has to be distilled in Tennessee from a mash which is at least 51 percent of *some* grain, distilled at less than 160 proof. While the predominant grain doesn't technically have to be corn (as it does in the case of Bourbon) in fact all Tennessee whiskey now made *is* at least 51 percent corn. Tennessee whiskey is an individual *kind* of whiskey, and Jack Daniel's and George Dickel are Tennessee Whiskeys—just as Wild Turkey and Jim Beam are each Kentucky Bourbons.

A common mistake made by newcomers and long-time devotees alike is to think that what makes Tennessee Whiskey so special and different is that it is a 'sour mash' whiskey; however, although Tennessee Whiskey is a sour mash so are all Kentucky Bourbons now made. We even have one friend to whom we gave a bottle of Jack Daniel's Black Label after our visit to Tennessee. This friend, a long-time Bourbon drinker, replied good-naturedly, "Oh, this is some of that sour mash stuff. I'd rather have some real Bourbon." This reaction is typical of the common confusion. There may be other reasons to prefer one kind of whiskey to the other, but all Bourbons and all Tennessee Whiskeys are made by the sour mash method.

The Lincoln County Process

The earliest description for making what we now call Tennessee Whiskey in Tennessee was whiskey made by 'the Lincoln County Process.' (Moore county, in which Lynchburg and Jack Daniel's Old Time Distillery are located, was once a part of Lincoln County.) Now exactly what was the 'Lincoln County Process' for making whiskey? There is evidence that as early as 1825 Alfred Eaton used maple charcoal to 'mellow' the whiskey made at his distillery in Tullahoma. It is this special charcoal mellowing (or leeching) part of the process which involves passing the new whiskey through several feet of maple charcoal which is what distinguishes Tennessee Whiskey as a unique kind of whiskey.

Eaton is usually credited with being the originator of this 'Lincoln County Process'; however, papers recently discovered at the Fileon club (the historical society in Kentucky) belonging to the Beall family, an early pioneering family in Kentucky, indicate that the charcoal mellowing process which is now distinctive of Tennessee whiskey, was being used in Kentucky as early as 1815–20. There is a full description and even a diagram of the process in the papers. So, while Eaton used the charcoal mellowing process, he obviously was not the first to use it. Why the mellowing process caught on in Tennessee and not in Kentucky is one of those puzzles about the early history of whiskey-making which remains unsolved. However and whenever and wherever it first started, it was this charcoal mellowing process which came to identify whiskey made by the Lincoln County Process in the mid-nineteenth century.

The Lincoln County Process was described as 'slow.' According to local folklore, using the Lincoln County process meant that 'it took a little longer to make the best whiskey.' What this meant is hard to say. Did the slow part of the process simply involve the added time necessary to drip the whiskey through the maple charcoal or did it also involve aging? Perhaps aging was an original part of the Lincoln County process, but it is unlikely that we can ever determine whether it was or not. Aging the whiskey in charred barrels is another step which now is part of what defines Tennessee Whiskey. Such aging takes time and also imparts a distinctive character to the whiskey. Interestingly, Lincoln County was sub-divided into smaller counties just as Bourbon County was in Kentucky, *but* Lincoln county was sub-divided before the designation of 'Lincoln County Whiskey' became widely known. Otherwise, today, we might have Bourbon whiskey (named after Bourbon County in Kentucky) and Lincoln Whiskey (named after Lincoln County in Tennessee).

The IRS Gets Involved

Jack Daniel's Distillery deserves the credit for convincing the federal government to recognize Tennessee Whiskey as officially different from Bourbon. This special distinction was endorsed by the Commissioner of the Internal Revenue Service in 1941. Reagor Motlow, eldest son of Lem Motlow, took samples of Jack Daniel's whiskey to Washington, D.C., with an explanation of the special leeching and mellowing process during which the new whiskey passes through several feet of hard maple charcoal before it is put into the charred oak barrels for aging. The Commissioner of the Internal Revenue responded with a letter in which he says that Jack Daniel's whiskey has "neither the characteristics of bourbon or rye whiskey" and that Tennessee Whiskey is "a distinctive product which may be labelled whiskey." It was this decision by the Internal Revenue Service which established Tennessee as a special *kind of whiskey*. Earlier, labels on Jack Daniel's whiskey had described it as a Bourbon.

It is this special step in the process, this 'mellowing' of the whiskey by slowing dripping it through several feet of maple charcoal to leech out undesirable congeners *before* the whiskey is put into barrels for aging, that earns it the special designation of 'Tennessee Whiskey.' In the folksy description of Roger Brashears at Jack Daniel's, the charcoal filtering takes "the hog tracks" out of the whiskey and gives it a head start on aging. "We always knew that we were different," Brashears says, "but it took the federal government from 1866 to 1941 to figure it out."

Jack Daniel's
Old Time Distillery

Before the time of mega-corporations and conglomerates, the success or failure of early business enterprises in America was primarily dependent upon *individuals*. In many cases, the vision, determination, and hard work of a single individual was the principle ingredient of a success story, and in no other case is the story of the success of a company more identified with the story of its founder and owner than in the case of Jack Daniel's Old Time Distillery in Lynchburg, Tennessee. The story of Jack Daniel is an interesting and unusual one indeed.

Young Jack Daniel

Jack Daniel, one of the undisputed giants of whiskey-making, spent the first few years of his life being known as a runt. Jasper Newton Daniel was born in 1846 in Lincoln County, Tennessee, as the youngest of ten children of Calaway and Lucinda Cook Daniel. In a practice which is common in the South, he was called by the diminutive, 'Jackie Boy.' According to the story, at age six, Jack Daniel, showing the gritty determination which was to make him a household name throughout much of the world, left home and went to live with a neighbor, 'Uncle' Felix Waggoner. Although Felix Waggoner was not really Jack's uncle and although neither Felix nor his wife, Huldah were even related to the Daniel family, he took 'Jackie Boy' in and raised him as his own son.

Jack Daniel Learns to Make Whiskey

After staying with Felix and Huldah Waggoner for barely a year, young Jack Daniel went to live with and work for Dan and Mary Jane Call, an enterprising young business couple who owned a general store. More importantly, Dan Call also owned and operated a

Jack Daniel

Courtesy of Jack Daniel's

whiskey still on Louse Creek, and he sold the whiskey in his general store. Young Jack learned to read and write, and how to run a retail business from the Calls. He also learned the details of how to make and sell whiskey at a very early age. Meanwhile, Jack was saving money.

Jack Daniel Goes Into Business

In 1859, when Jack Daniel was 13 years old, Dan Call, a lay Lutheran preacher, decided that he could no longer continue in the whiskey business. At the time, the Temperance Movement was gathering strength across the country, and Call was pressured by family and friends alike to sell the still. Jack Daniel took over the operation of the Call still when he was only 13, and because Dan Call would no longer sell whiskey in his general store, young Jack Daniel started making long wagon trips to sell his whiskey in Huntsville, Alabama, the temporary state capital and one of the largest cities in the state at the time. Jack's trips continued throughout the Civil War when Huntsville was occupied by Union soldiers. Few details are known about Jack's trips to Huntsville, probably because selling whiskey to troops was illegal, and Jack 'smuggled' his whiskey to Huntsville. Given the nature of the times, great fortunes were made or lost, and during this time, young Jack Daniel thrived. He was 18 when the Civil War ended, and he was well on his way to accumulating not only financial wealth but also a wealth of experience and success as an entrepreneur.

The Move to Lynchburg and Cave Spring Hollow

Following the Civil War, Jack Daniel quickly moved into a bigger and better operation with his distillery. Having paid off his debt to Dan Call, Jack realized the importance of being near the new railroad which had just made its way into Tullahoma. He entered into a brief partnership with Colonel John Mason Hughes, a Civil War hero, freshly home from the war, and moved all of his equipment from the site of Call's Still on Louse Creek to the Hughes plantation near Lynchburg, increasing the capacity of his operation at the same time. However, soon after setting up operations on the property of Colonel Hughes, Jack discovered that property beside Cave Spring in what was known as 'The Hollow' in Lynchburg was available. He immediately leapt at the opportunity to lease this property because of its water from a deep underground spring. This water was considered pure, with absolutely no iron in it. The crystal clear water arrived at ground level at a constant 56 degrees Fahrenheit year round—summer and winter—perfect for making whiskey. Jack Daniel moved his entire operation to Cave Spring in 1866 and once again increased the size of his operation.

Evidently Jack Daniel learned to make whiskey using the 'Lincoln County Method' from Dan Call when he first learned how to make whiskey in the early 1850s, but there are no records which indicated exactly when Jack Daniel first started using the charcoal "mellowing" step. It is also difficult to determine exactly when Jack

James Harris

The cave with its source of limestone water for Jack Daniel's whiskey

Daniel began aging his whiskey and for how long. Nor are there records which indicate when Jack Daniel first started using charred barrels for the aging. Perhaps he did from the very beginning, and perhaps this also was a part of the original Lincoln County Process.

The Oldest Registered Distillery?

When the United States Federal Government began to impose licensing and tax restrictions upon distilleries following the Civil War, many distillers resisted this claim of the federal government to regulate and control what they considered a natural part of their daily lives. United States Federal 'revenue agents' received a hostile welcome throughout Tennessee, Kentucky, and the rest of the South. According to the way in which the story is told in and around Lynchburg, Jack Daniel was a man of both vision and opportunity and recognizing the inevitability (and perhaps the marketing advantage) of becoming the very first distillery to be officially registered by the United Sates government, Jack Daniel hurriedly completed all of the forms necessary to register the distillery and rushed to Washington, D.C., to complete the process. According to the story,

Jack Daniel's Distillery became the very first distillery legally registered to produce whiskey in the United States in 1866. Jack Daniel's
now makes great use of the 'No. 1' designation which it currently
holds from the Bureau of the Internal Revenue Service and of its
claim to be the "oldest registered distillery in the United States."
Presently a plaque on the wall of Jack Daniel's original office proudly
informs visitors of these claims to fame as well as the fact that the
distillery has been added to the National Register of Historical Places
by the Department of the Interior.

There is no doubt that Jack Daniel's is deserving of some distinction in terms of its registration; however, it is difficult to determine exactly what that distinction is. Uncovering the true story of
the 'No. 1' designation requires a bit of historical sleuthing. It is
true that the United States began to register distilleries following
the Civil War, but, so far as we have been able to determine, even
though this was a federal requirement, there was never a single,
national registration of distilleries. The registration was done by
regions, and there were sometimes more than one region in a particular state. For example, George Dickel is now designated 'No. 2,'
but, of course, that means the second distillery operating *in Tennessee.* The Burnheim Distillery in Louisville is designated 'No. 1,' but
that means number one in Kentucky. Toward the end of the nineteenth century, according to Goodspeed's *History of Tennessee,* there
were almost 700 licensed distilleries operating in Tennessee and 15
in Moore County alone. In the Midas Financial Index Directory for
1911 (copyrighted 1910, the year that prohibition began in Tennessee), Jack Daniel's is listed as Distillery No. 514, and George Dickel
is listed as Distillery No. 392. In that same year, Jack Daniel's moved
to St. Louis, and the Jack Daniel's Distillery in St. Louis (at 4000
Duncan Avenue) became Distillery No. 1 *for the District of Missouri.*

When national Prohibition ended in 1933 and Jack Daniel's returned its operations to Lynchburg, Tennessee, it was the first distillery to be licensed to make whiskey in Tennessee following Prohibition so it retained its 'No. 1' designation although the meaning
had shifted from 'No. 1 in Missouri' to 'No. 1 in Tennessee.' When
the George Dickel Distillery was rebuilt in 1958, it became 'No. 2'
which means, of course, 'No. 2 in Tennessee.' The side of the label

on a bottle of Jack Daniel's still proclaims that Jack Daniel's is "The oldest registered distillery in the United States." As we have seen, this probably does not mean that Jack Daniel's was the *first* distillery registered in the United States.

Jack Daniel, Entrepreneur and Businessman

Whatever number is actually to assigned to the distillery Jack Daniel must nonetheless be credited with the keen sense of a very savvy businessman. When the distillery was registered in 1866, Jack Daniel was barely 20 years old. In the next few years he continued to develop and expand the business which he had acquired and built. When labels and then bottling were required by the United States Government, Jack Daniel seized upon what many regarded as unwelcome intrusions as great opportunities to promote and advertise his whiskey. Capitalizing upon the importance of tradition for Tennesseans, his labels made constant use of the designation 'Old.' The distillery became known as the 'Jack Daniel Old Time Distillery,' and the whiskey became known as 'Old Time No. 7' which is now 'Old No. 7.' The origin of Old Time No. 7 is supposedly traceable to a business friend in Tullahoma who owned a well-known chain of seven retail stores and had successfully made use of that fact in promoting his goods. These designations were proudly stencilled on the barrels leaving the distilleries for distant markets—which now included Nashville and even Memphis and St. Louis.

Jack Daniel, Country Squire

When he was still in his early twenties, Jack Daniel was an accomplished businessman and also something of a dandy and country squire. Standing either five feet two inches or five feet five inches, depending upon the source, he regularly dressed in a dark, knee-length frock coat and a white planter's hat, and he sported a mustache and a goatee. He loved the good life, and became widely known for his charms and generosity. He hosted large parties at his mansion, just outside Lynchburg, and organized and outfitted the

Lynchburg Silver Cornet Band, a band of locals who performed at all local events and remained active until World War I.

The White Rabbit and the Red Dog

We have seen earlier how saloon life dominated the social life at the end of the nineteenth century. It is not surprising then that in 1892, Jack Daniel opened two saloons in Lynchburg: The White Rabbit and The Red Dog. While the explanation of the origin of these names is now lost, we can speculate that 'The White Rabbit' was derived from Louis Carroll's *Alice in Wonderland*. Perhaps there was a favorite dog of Jack Daniel's which happened to be red; however, 'The Red Dog' was more likely a clever way of naming (and advertising) his whiskey. We have learned earlier that the raw whiskey fresh out of the doubler is called 'white dog' and the aged whiskey, once it has taken on its distinctive red coloring from the charred barrels was called 'red eye' so perhaps, 'The Red Dog' was simply another designation for the whiskey which Jack Daniel made and sold in his saloons. When glass bottles came into use in the 1890s, Jack Daniel chose a distinctive square bottle for his product, and, except for special bottlings, the square bottles have remained in use to the present day.

Gold Medals

In 1904 Jack Daniel's Old Time No. 7 Whiskey was awarded a gold medal for the best whiskey at the World's Fair in St. Louis (also known as the Louisiana Purchase Exposition). Jack Daniel made great use of this award in promoting his whiskey (Jack Daniel's Old No. 7 was also to win gold medals at international competitions at world fairs in 1913, 1914, and 1954). He issued an elaborate and expensive special 'Gold Medal' bottling in tall round bottles with fluted sides and white embossed lettering on the bottle which proclaimed "Jack Daniel's Gold Medal Whiskey." This special bottling is just one example of the energetic marketing which Jack Daniel used to promote his product. As far as we can determine, Jack Daniel was the first to use special bottlings as a way of attracting attention to his whiskey. He earlier had done special private bottlings with different ornate and elaborate bottles for his Belle of Lincoln and the Centennial Bottle issued in 1896 to commemorate the 100th anniversary of Tennessee's statehood. In 1907, Jack Daniel issued a special bottling called the Maxwell House Decanter which was named after the famous hotel and bar in Nashville. (It was at the Maxwell House during a visit that President Teddy Roosevelt is supposed to have described the Maxwell House coffee as "good to the last drop"—an early American product, noted for quality, which along with Jack Daniel's Old No. 7, has endured to the present day.) Over the years, Jack Daniel's Old Time Distillery has continued the practice of special bottlings and has produced hundreds of different special decanters which now have become favorite gift selections and collectors' items for many people.

Lem Motlow

Since Jack Daniel never married, his nephew Lem Motlow, who had begun working for Jack Daniel in 1887, took over the distillery when Jack Daniel died in 1911. The glowing eulogies which appeared in various newspapers revealed Jack Daniel to be a much beloved and respected figure. When the state of Tennessee went dry in 1910, ten years earlier than national Prohibition, Lem Motlow moved the distillery to St. Louis, and it continued in operation there until 1919. Although several distilleries remained in operation during prohibition to produce medicinal whiskey, Jack Daniel's Old Time Distillery did not operate during this period. Lem Motlow returned to Lynchburg and developed a national reputation as a mule- and horse-breeder. He was also elected to the Tennessee House of Representatives for two terms and then to the Tennessee State Senate for two terms. Although Tennessee remained dry following Repeal in 1933, Lem Motlow was successful in getting the Tennessee state legislature to pass a bill allowing the manufacture of whiskey in the state. A local referendum in Moore County later narrowly passed, and Jack Daniel's Old Time distillery was finally able to resume operations in 1938.

Lem Motlow

Courtesy of Jack Daniel's

The trials and tribulations which faced Lem Motlow in restarting the Jack Daniel's Distillery in Lynchburg are illustrative of what a lot of distillers must have experienced. First, in 1931, Lem Motlow resisted the attempt by the Schenley Corporation in Kentucky (Schenley Products Company) to take over the name of 'Jack Daniel.' After all, at the time, the Jack Daniel name had not been used in whiskey distilling for over ten years, and so far as Schenley was concerned it seemed that Jack Daniel's Distillery was out of business for good. After a protracted legal battle (the lawyers always seem to get involved), Lem Motlow was able to keep the control and rights to the name of 'Jack Daniel'—primarily, it seems, because even though the name had not been used in connection with whiskey during Prohibition, Lem Motlow had conducted his mule and horse breeding and selling business under the name of 'the Jack Daniel Company'!

Just three years later, Lem Motlow was still trying to secure the financial backing to reopen the distillery. Evidently, some potential investors had backed out on their promises to provide financing (imagine how the descendants of those investors would feel today if they knew). Lem Motlow wrote back to the Schenley Company asking if they would like to join him in an "equitable proposition" in running the Jack Daniel Distillery. The people at Schenley decided that they were not interested. If they had thought differently, United Distillers (which bought Schenley and which now owns George Dickel) would own part of Jack Daniel's too. In 1936, Lem Motlow allowed the Jack Daniel label to be used, on some whiskey which had been stored in St. Louis, for a "royalty," and again offered the same sort of arrangement to Schenley. Apparently, this is how Lem Motlow raised the necessary capital to reopen the Jack Daniel's Distillery in Lynchburg.

It took a person of exceptionally strong will and character to save Jack Daniel's Distillery and to get it back into operation again. This was a crucial chapter in one of America's great success stories.

Brown-Forman

Lem Motlow preserved the Jack Daniel's Old Time Distillery after the death of Jack Daniel and during Prohibition. His four sons continued operation of the distillery after Lem Motlow's death in 1947 and increased the size of the operation by building new warehouses for storing the whiskey on the hills surrounding The Hollow. Jack Daniel's Distillery was sold to Brown-Forman Distiller Corporation of Louisville in 1956 for a reported twenty million dollars. Brown-Forman, one of the oldest and most respected businesses in the industry, was started in 1870 in Louisville and now includes Old Forester Bourbon among its products along with, of course, Jack Daniel's.

Making Jack Daniel's Whiskey

One of the 'secrets' of the consistently high quality of Jack Daniel's whiskey is the pure limestone water drawn from deep in Cave Spring for both mashing and reducing the proof strength of the whiskey before bottling. It was primarily for this limitless supply of pure limestone water that Jack Daniel first moved the distillery here.

There are 48 stainless steel fermenters at Jack Daniel's, and each one holds 48,000 gallons of mash, and they are all used in a year-round operation. This is, of course, a sour mash operation with about 25 percent set-back which is returned to each new mashing from the previous one.

The formula at Jack Daniel's is no secret, and is the same for both the Green and Black Labels. It calls for 80 percent corn, twelve percent rye, and eight percent barley malt. The process starts with very selective, clean grains from a small group of suppliers. The corn is cooked first—at atmospheric pressure, not in pressure cookers—at 212–215 degrees Fahrenheit for about 45 minutes. It must then be cooled, we were told by Gerald Hamilton, the Distillery Technical Manager, to approximately 168 degrees Fahrenheit, before adding the rye, to prevent the rye from clumping. Reducing the temperature again and adding the barley malt is the last step in the fermentation process.

Distillation takes place in the all-copper Vendome beer still. The whiskey first passes through the beer still and then through the doubler where it emerges at 140 proof. The new whiskey, the white dog, then enters directly into the charcoal mellowing process. After aging, the proof is lowered to 115 or 125 degrees (depending upon who the source is) before the whiskey is put into barrels for aging.

The special charcoal mellowing process, distinctive of Tennessee Whiskey, involves slowly dripping through twelve feet deep stainless steel vats. The maple charcoal is prepared at the distillery in an open-air firing of stacks of split maple logs. As dramatic a spectacle as the firing is, it is not a complete process of combustion. Some of the sugars in the wood remain in the charcoal and are partly responsible for the distinctive flavor of Jack Daniel's products.

It takes from four to five days for the whiskey to pass through this additional step in the process. However, once the vats are charged with whiskey and the flow is established, there is a con-

Maple charcoal, used in the charcoal mellowing process

Courtesy of Jack Daniel's

tinuous supply of whiskey from the bottom of the vats, and there is no additional delay in the production process. Yet, this step is expensive in other ways because some of the whiskey remains in the charcoal. Gerald Hamilton estimates that as much as three or four percent of the total output of the distillery is lost in this process. The used charcoal briquettes, when they are replaced, are packaged and sold to the public for barbecue grilling.

Aging

There are 48 warehouses at Jack Daniel's Old Time Distillery. The warehouses are located both in the hollow surrounding the distillery itself and on the hillside around the hollow where they may well be the first thing which a visitor to Lynchburg sees. Each ware-house has a capacity of over 20,000 barrels each. Since each barrel contains 50 gallons or more of whiskey, a little simple arithmetic reveals that when the warehouses are full (which they are most of the time), there are something close to *50 million gallons* of Jack Daniel's whiskey gentle mellowing in the Tennessee countryside at any given time. Jack Daniel's still maintains the labor-intensive in-vestment of rotating the barrels as they age in the warehouses. Pe-riodically, the barrels are rotated by hand to ensure that, over a long period of time, the different barrels age uniformly.

Jack Daniel's Black Label

The distillery now produces four products: Jack Daniel's Green Label, Jack Daniel's Black Label, Lem Motlow, and Gentleman Jack. Although there are no ages indicated on either of the bottlings of Jack Daniel's, both are said to spend at least four years in the bar-rel. The Green Label is bottled at 86.4 proof, and the more familiar and more popular Black Label is bottled at 86 proof for most do-mestic markets and at 90 proof for foreign markets. Lem Motlow is sold only in restricted markets as a one-year old, 90 proof whiskey. The differences between all of these whiskeys is accounted for in terms of age and proof since according to our information, the same formula is used for all of these whiskeys.

Black Label is the most popular product and arguably one of the world's most successful products at achieving name recogni-tion. The Black Label still appears in the same familiar square bottle with a rounded, fluted neck with "Jack Daniel's Tennessee Whis-key" in bold white lettering on the distinctive black label.

The list of seven gold medals awarded to Jack Daniel's are listed on the side of the label, along with the two proud claims "Made in Tennessee" and "Bottled at the Distillery"—a not-so-subtle rebuke aimed at George Dickel since Dickel is trucked in bulk to Kentucky where it is bottled. "Jack Daniel's Old Time, Old No. 7" appears twice on the cap and again, very prominently, on the front of the label, and the claim as "The Oldest Registered Distillery in the United

States" is repeated on the side of the label. Lem Motlow is still indicated as being the "Proprietor" of the distillery although he died in 1947 and although the distillery was sold to Brown-Forman in 1956.

1895 Replica

A more recent example of the marketing genius of Jack Daniel's is the recent issue of an 1895 replica bottling. The replica comes in a one liter size in the clear square design of the original with the rounded, fluted neck and "old Time Distillery, No. 7, Jack Daniel, Distiller, Lynchburg, Tennessee" embossed on the clear glass. There is no label. The whiskey is 86 proof, presumably the same as the Black Label. A further aspect of this marketing strategy is a removable tag which allows customers to register their 'limited quantity' bottlings with the distillery by mailing a return form to the distillery by mail. Another of Jack Daniel's adroit marketing schemes, it certainly creates a special bond with the customers. We mailed our registration right away. Our bottle was numbered 106922.

Gentleman Jack

Gentleman Jack is the newest product from the Jack Daniel's Old Time Distillery and is an attempt to compete with the up-scale, single-malt Scotch whiskies and the single-barrel and small-batch Bourbons. It comes at 80 proof and is the result of a formula different from 'Old No. 7.' This formula is a trade secret. 'Gentleman Jack,' an allusion, of course, to Jack Daniel, Gentleman and Squire, is described as a "*Rare* Tennessee Whiskey" and a "single whiskey." Exactly what this designation means in the case of a Tennessee Whiskey is not clear. The label proclaims that it is "not a combination of whiskies" curiously using the Scottish spelling for the plural while retaining the distinctively American spelling for the singular. The appellation 'single whiskey' cannot retain any of the meaning which it has in the case of single-malt Scotch whiskies, and it does not mean 'single-barrel' as with such single-barrel Bourbons as

Blanton's, Hancock, Elmer Lee, and Rock Hill Farm from Leestown Distillers or Kentucky Spirit from Wild Turkey. After trying for some time to sort out this matter, we have been able to determine from the distillery that 'single whiskey' used to describe Gentleman Jack really simply means 'straight whiskey' in the way in which 'straight Bourbon' means that it is not blended with grain alcohol. But, of course, all Tennessee Whiskey is single whiskey in this sense, including not only Jack Daniel's Green Label and Black Label but the George Dickel labels too, since all Tennessee Whiskey by definition must be straight whiskey. So we can ignore this entirely redundant claim. The whiskey is good enough to stand on its own without the addition of empty hyperbole. The most unique thing about Gentleman Jack is that it goes through a second charcoal filtering *after* aging and before bottling. The exact nature of this process is patented and secret, one of the very few things at the distillery which visitors are not allowed to see, but we have a fair estimation of the nature of the process. As we have described above, the first charcoal filtering (which both Jack Daniel's and George Dickel prefer to call a process of 'mellowing'), which gives Tennessee Whiskey its identity as a unique *kind* of whiskey, occurs in large open vats, two stories high, where the whiskey enters at the top and then, some time later, exits at the bottom. Our best guess is that, in the second charcoal filtering, the whiskey passes through a pipe (or a much smaller container) which contains the charcoal, and that it passes through much more quickly than in the first charcoal mellowing. Whatever the exact nature of the process, it must be a very delicate filtering since the color of the whiskey is unchanged. While we are not sure about the time this process takes or its exact nature, we are much more sure about the results—which are very pronounced.

Y'all Come Back Now

In our experience, the people involved in the whiskey distilling industry are among the most friendly people we have ever met. The people at Jack Daniel's Old Time Distillery are no exception. Visitors are not only welcomed but encouraged at the distillery, and on any given day with the parking lot filled to capacity, the number of visitors usually far exceeds the number of permanent residents of Lynchburg (still advertised as only 361). The accommodations for visitors at the distillery are as elaborate as any we found. There is a large comfortable waiting area with guided tours which leave every half-hour. Lemonade is served in a replica of Jack Daniel's White Rabbit Saloon after the tour. This is down-home atmosphere at its best. Don't expect samples of any products of Jack Daniel's since Moore County is dry; however, in just the last year special souvenir bottles of Jack Daniel's are now sold at the Visitors Center at the distillery. This is a special bottling of Jack Daniel's whiskey in a special fluted decanter which comes in a protective wooden box. This bottling is called Jack Daniel's Barrel House 1.

The Town of Lynchburg

At the Lynchburg Hardware and General Store, a short walk away on the town square in Lynchburg, there is a large souvenir shop with a great variety of Jack Daniel's memorabilia—everything from clocks, mirrors, playing cards, glasses, and jugs to the ubiquitous T-shirts and ball caps. Although Lynchburg is a tiny town, composed almost completely of the town square, visitors have the great fortune of being able to choose from several local restaurants which specialize in down-home Southern cooking. Our favorite is Miss Bobo's Boarding House, just one block off the main square. Miss Bobo's serves a casual, family-style dinner (that's 'lunch' for Yankees) each day with two different meats and lots of homegrown vegetables, home-made bread, and desserts. Huge platters and bowls of food are placed on the table and refilled when needed.

Visitors at Jack Daniel's

During our visit we were struck by the close identification which visitors had with Jack Daniel's. When we arrived, at nine o'clock on a Monday morning, the parking lot was already half-full, and on our walk to the entrance we passed cars from Tennessee, Georgia,

Arkansas, California, Mississippi, Florida, Indiana, Wisconsin, Virginia, Ohio, Illinois, Pennsylvania, New Jersey, and Quebec. There are special facilities for pets and special parking for tour buses. Visitors come in large numbers and include everyone from bikers to entire families with children and occasional families with three generations. Their excitement and enthusiasm were matched by a kind of reverence and affection which we found unmatched in any of our other visits to distilleries. People *arrive* for the tour of Jack Daniel's Old Time Distillery wearing Jack Daniel's T-shirts and caps—*before* they visit the souvenir shop, and they proudly display their affiliation with Jack Daniel's as they pose for family photographs in front of various parts of the distillery. A pilgrimage to the distillery for many of them is a lifelong ambition.

This consumer loyalty is enhanced by a masterful marketing campaign with an annual budget of from six to eight million dollars. The marketing strategy has been successful in reinforcing the enormous product loyalty which probably explains why Jack Daniel's has avoided the declining sales which have been generally characteristic of 'brown whiskeys'—Scotch whiskies, Bourbons, and Tennessee Whiskeys—over the past several years. The distillery is in operation twelve months out of the year for five or sometimes six days a week and closes for cleaning and maintenance only for a couple of weeks each summer.

Part of the success of Jack Daniel's is to be accounted for by the simplicity and consistency of its operations. Jack Daniel's makes very few products, the products have the same name as the distillery at which they are made, and they have kept their operations at the same place. The effectiveness of the marketing of Jack Daniel's seems to be attributed to their success in getting directly in contact with the American public, the consumers themselves, and they do it with a personal touch. The distillery invests a lot of time and resources in public relations, and inquiries to the distillery, by phone or letter, always receive a personal response. Real people—not actors—are used in all of Jack Daniel's advertisements, and people are invited in the advertisements to visit the distillery or to write if they can't come for a visit. We highly recommend a visit to Jack Daniel's and to Lynchburg. Plan to send the entire day there. The distillery is located off Highway 55 as it enters Lynchburg. Lynchburg is located just 13 miles from Tullahoma and about halfway between 165 and 124 some 65–70 miles south of Nashville.

TASTING NOTES

Jack Daniel's Old Time No. 7, Black Label

A very smooth and refined whiskey. The charcoal filtering process removes the fieriness which characterizes some straight Bourbons and leaves a cleaner, lighter whiskey. We find a faint hint of the charcoal—a smoky, almost peaty flavor. Perhaps because of the cleaner taste, the vanilla tones from the aging process in the charred barrels are more distinctive—a feature we also noticed with the whiskeys from George Dickel.

Gentleman Jack

Not only a 'Rare Tennessee Whiskey' as the label claims, it is a rare whiskey of any description. This is an extraordinarily smooth whiskey which (for the most part) retains the character and complexity of the Jack Daniel's Black Label although we feel that the body and the texture are noticeably lighter. Perhaps some of the complexity of the flavor has been sacrificed here for the exceptional smoothness, but the flavor which remains, though lighter, is still full of depth and character. We thought that some of the smoothness might be accounted for by the lower proof; however, we tried reducing the Jack Daniel's Black Label to 80 proof by adding pure spring water and could not match the smoothness of Gentleman Jack. Neat or on the rocks, but this is not a whiskey to be used in mixes.

George Dickel Distillery

George Dickel Distillery is located in a little unincorporated town called Normandy, in Cascade Hollow, just a few miles out of Tullahoma, Tennessee, a town of under 20,000 people. In fact, George Dickel is closer to Tullahoma than is the Jack Daniel's Distillery to Lynchburg. Today, Tullahoma has suffered the fate of many other small towns in the United States. The downtown area is fighting to maintain its integrity, and the suburbs, filled with people who work at the nearby Arnold Engineering Development Center, run by the United States Air Force, and the University of Tennessee Space Institute, have moved farther and farther out. The town is locked in a constant struggle to keep its population and tax base.

Tullahoma and the Railroad

From its beginning in 1851 through the mid-twentieth century, Tullahoma was a dynamic and thriving metropolitan area. Tens of thousands of people visited or passed through Tullahoma in the late nineteenth century—a claim unrivalled by any but the largest metropolitan areas. Tullahoma had two main attractions—the railroad and pure limestone water.

Tullahoma is not an old town by American standards or even by Tennessee standards. It owes its establishment, its early success and its very life to the railroad. The town was established as a major center for the Nashville and Chattanooga Railroad, and the town grew around the railroad—so much so that most of the families in town were connected to the railroad in one way on another. This was at a time when the men and their families who made up the 'crews' for a particular train were all located in a particular town by the railroad.

The rail line from Tullahoma connected to the main line in McMinnville, Tennessee, and for more than a half-century, the crews for a particular train would work only a particular run—from

Tullahoma to McMinnville and then back again. Author Harris, whose grandfather and great-uncle were a conductor and an engineer on the Tullahoma to McMinnville run, remembers being allowed to ride in the engineer's seat of the great steam locomotive as it roared along.

The railroad remained a major factor in the identity of Tullahoma until the mid-twentieth century, and the importance of the railroad provides some historical insight into what life was like in small towns across America and the ways in which small town and rural families survived the Great Depression. Harris's father, who was born and grew up in Tullahoma, recounted the story of how, as a child, he would catch the train on which his father served as a conductor and his uncle as an engineer each afternoon after school for the run from Tullahoma to McMinnville. The young boy would study his lessons until the train was near McMinnville; then, he would gather all of the eggs which the chickens had laid while they were on the train and being shipped to parts unknown for slaughter. The eggs provided a major contribution to the support of the family during a very difficult time when every member of the family, including the children, were expected to contribute.

Understanding the importance of the railroad also provides us with some explanations for the way in which this country mobilized for World War II. Camp Forrest (named for Confederate Nathan Bedford Forrest from Tullahoma), one of the largest induction centers on the east coast of the United States, was established just outside Tullahoma. Now why, the modern reader might wonder, would the Army put one of the largest and most important induction centers way off in the middle of Tennessee? The answer is simple— because of the railroad. From Camp Forrest, troops could be shipped, by railroad, to all points, from Maine to California.

If the people in the town of Tullahoma did not work for the railroad, they provided the goods and services for those who did. The railroad ran right through the middle of the town with two-way streets on either side of the track, and all of the town's shops and stores located alongside. From the late eighteenth century onwards, Tullahoma boasted of the widest Main Street in the country. In fact, even today the casual visitor can buy postcards with an aerial view of main street, with the railroad tracks in the middle, and the description "Widest Main Street in the U.S.A." Ironically, today there is no railroad passenger service to Tullahoma. Only freight trains pass through this town, which was established by the railroad for the railroad.

Limestone Water and Tullahoma

The second main attraction Tullahoma had to offer was its water, and in the mid-nineteenth century this was an important attraction. Although there are no records to confirm this, it makes sense to infer that the railroad first came to Tullahoma because of the water. The pure and plentiful limestone water was important for two reasons: first, it provided the source of the attraction which made Tullahoma a major health resort in the last part of the nineteenth century. The many springs of 'mineral water' attracted tens of thousands of people, who came to Tullahoma mostly by train, to bathe in the healing waters there. Secondly, the pure limestone water provided the iron-free water necessary for making whiskey. And make it they did. At the turn of the twentieth century, Tullahoma could probably boast of more distilleries within a ten-mile radius that any other place in the world. For example, *The Goodspeed History of Tennessee* says that there were eight operating distilleries in and around Tullahoma in 1886. At least three of these were in Cascade Hollow. The limestone water, the life-blood of whiskey making, which is found in Tullahoma and the surrounding area, were to attract the best and the best-known whiskey makers in Tennessee, including, as we shall see, George Dickel. Since the detailed accounts are not available, one can only imagine how the fame of Tennessee Whiskey, as well as samples of the product itself, were spread far and wide by the many visitors to Tullahoma during this period. Trains brought visitors to Tullahoma from all points of the compass and carried the visitors away again along with shipments of Tennessee Whiskey. Once again we see how whiskey is interwoven with the economic and cultural development of this country in the nineteenth century.

George Dickel as a Young Man.

The story of George Dickel Distillery is the story of the man George Dickel. The nineteenth century in America was a time at which aggressive, talented, and strong-willed individuals established industries and fortunes which made them legendary. George Dickel was one of these individuals. He was born in Germany in 1818, in Gruenburg, near Frankfort-on-the-Main, to a family of grain millers. George was not the eldest son, so perhaps it was a desire for opportunity that led him to make his way as a young man to the United States and to Nashville, Tennessee. Although the exact dates of his immigration are not known, his obituary in 1894, indicated that he had been a citizen of the United States for over 50 years so he must have made his way to this country at least by 1844, at the age of 26.

One can only imagine the difficulties faced by a young German immigrant in central Tennessee in the mid-nineteenth century; however, by 1853, Dickel had founded his mercantile business in Nashville. It was probably through selling whiskey in his wholesale business that George Dickel first established connections with the whiskey industry. By 1866, he was selling some whiskey retail, and by 1870, George Dickel had married Augusta, a native Tennessean, and had become a "retail liquor dealer." He then established the firm of George A. Dickel and Company.

Cascade Distillery

Cascade Distillery was founded near Cascade Spring and Cascade Falls on the hillside of what was known as Cascade Hollow in 1877 by John F. Brown and F.E. Cunningham. There was at least one other distillery, a sawmill and a grist mill in the same area taking advantage of the same water and gravity power.

The early history of Cascade Distillery is a story which, like Dickens's *Tale of Two Cities,* is a combination of "the best of times" and "the worst of times." By the end of the nineteenth century, the Temperance League and the national movement towards Prohibition had gained enormous strength and influence. As part of the

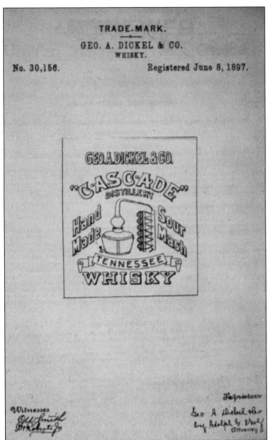

*Trademark
application of
George Dickel*

Courtesy fo United Distllers

Southern Bible Belt, Tennessee was way ahead of the curve in re-
stricting both the manufacture and the sale of whiskey. In 1887, the
extension of Tennessee's 'Four Mile Act' effectively eliminated all
retail sales of whiskey in rural parts of Tennessee. This was not the
best of times to start a new distillery in Tennessee. However, Cascade Distillery apparently thrived, and in 1888 Victor Schwab,
George Dickel's partner and brother-in-law, acquired a controlling
interest in the Cascade Distillery. As a result, George A. Dickel
and Co. acquired the sole right to bottle and distribute Cascade
Whiskey, and the names of Dickel and Cascade become inextricably connected. The company began to promote the sale of Cascade
Tennessee Whiskey, and the business began to grow.

For the student of whiskey folklore and history, there are several interesting things about this period in the life of Cascade Distillery. The distillery was still named 'Cascade' as was all of the whiskey made there. George A. Dickel and Co. owned the distillery, but the Dickel name would not replace the Cascade name until much later. The labels on the bottles indicate that it was still the Cascade Distillery which was producing the whiskey, but that it was owned by Dickel. Labels from Cascade products during this period boldly proclaim that the product is "Tennessee Whisky." Exactly when this designation was first made by Cascade Distillery and for how long is impossible to determine, but this provides us with another interesting piece of the story we told in the early part of this chapter about how Tennessee Whiskey came to be legally recognized as a unique *kind* of whiskey. Although it was Jack Daniel's Old Time Distillery which was responsible for persuading the federal government to designate Tennessee Whiskey as a separate and distinct kind of whiskey in 1941 (at a time when neither Cascade Distillery or George Dickel Distillery was operating in Tennessee), it was apparently Cascade Distillery which first begin to designate and market its whiskey as "Tennessee Whisky" (using the Scottish spelling). During this time, the whiskey being made at Jack Daniel's Distillery was still known as a Bourbon.

These same labels of early Cascade Tennessee Whisky proudly proclaimed that this was "old style," "sour mash" whiskey. The labels also carried the trademark of George A. Dickel and Co. (for which the company received a patent in 1897) which shows a copper pot-still and the worm for condensing the alcohol. The application for the patent, made in 1895, indicates that the trademark had been in constant use by the George A. Dickel and Co. since 1870, on labels, barrels, circulars, and other advertisements.

George Dickel Dies

Ironically, during the time that George A. Dickel and Co. was thriving and acquiring the Cascade Distillery, George Dickel himself was slowly dying. He had suffered a fall from a horse in 1888, and although the exact nature of his injuries are not described in the family history, he never fully recovered from the injuries and died of resulting complications on June 11th, 1894. At the time of Dickel's death, the company which he had founded and which bore his name was Nashville's oldest surviving business to have operated continuously under the same name.

Victor Schwab and his son, George (named after George Dickel), continued to operate George A. Dickel and Co. and the Cascade Distillery. The distillery was still named the Cascade Distillery and the product was still called 'Tennessee Whisky.' The distillery was enlarged and modernized in 1904, and its capacity was increased to 150 bushels per day—making it the largest distillery operating in Tennessee. Business was booming, and it was the best of times for George A. Dickel and Co. However, the worst of times loomed on the horizon. The blowing wind of change had become the hurricane of Prohibition. In 1910 (when national Prohibition was still ten years away), just six years after the Cascade Distillery was made into the largest and most modern distillery in Tennessee, the state of Tennessee became dry, and all distilleries operating within the state were ordered closed.

In 1911, George A. Dickel and Co. moved the Dickel process to Louisville where Cascade 'Tennessee Whisky' continued, still using the 'leeching' through maple charcoal, to be made until 1919—something which would not be possible today since Tennessee Whiskey can now only be made legally in Tennessee. So, ironically, Cascade Tennessee Whisky was made in Kentucky. Meanwhile, faced with the apparent permanent prohibition in Tennessee and in need of capital to keep the business going, Victor Schwab sold the original site of the distillery in Cascade Hollow in 1917.

The Death and Rebirth of Cascade and George Dickel

From 1911 until 1937, Stitzel, in Louisville, Kentucky, was the location of the Dickel Distillery. Schwab leased the Dickel label to Stitzel-Weller. Stitzel-Weller, in turn, made and marketed Dickel, paying Schwab a royalty from the proceeds. In 1937 the name and the process were bought by Schenley for $100,000. This must have been confusing for anyone familiar with the earlier long history and close association of the names of 'Cascade' and 'Dickel' with Tennessee Whiskey, and one can only imagine what George Dickel himself would have thought of having the Cascade name used for a Kentucky Bourbon.

Finally, Schenley re-united the names of Cascade and Dickel by acquiring the rights to the name 'Cascade' and began making George Dickel's Cascade Whisky at the George T. Stagg Distillery in Frankfort, Kentucky. Schenley ordered that a new distillery be built in Cascade Hollow near the original site of the Cascade Distillery, and the new plant, called the Cascade Hollow Distillery, opened in 1958. The new distillery now uses the limestone water which emerges at a constant 60 degrees from the same Cascade Spring which supplied the original Cascade Distillery.

The first bottlings from the new distillery reached the market in 1964. The long time-lag here indicates the difficulty which any new distillery is faced with: it is several years before there is any return on the investment. At the time the distillery was built, Jack Daniel's was the only Tennessee Whiskey being made, and Schenley and then United Distillers must have had great confidence in the marketability of a second Tennessee Whiskey. Jack Daniel's was already

Courtesy of United Distillers

The George Dickel Distillery, 1992

well-established, as we have seen, as not only the sole Tennessee Whiskey, but as one of the most successful American products at name-recognition and market share.

Although George Dickel remains small today (it currently has 30 full-time employees and a maximum capacity of mashing 1,500 bushels of grain a day), it has certainly been successful at creating a niche for itself in a very competitive market, and its devotees are extremely loyal. The first bottlings from the new Cascade Hollow Distillery were still called 'Cascade Whisky,' but the name was changed to George Dickel Tennessee Whisky since Schenley was still using the Cascade name for a brand of Bourbon. The spelling of 'whisky' is not a mistake here. Even today George Dickel retains the Scottish spelling of 'whisky,' a practice which, as far as we can tell, has been consistent since the beginnings of the Cascade Distillery. This is a practice which is shared in the American whiskey industry only by Maker's Mark and Brown-Forman, both in Kentucky. Schenley was bought by Guinness in 1987, and the distillery is now owned by United Distillers. So, like the Phoenix, the Cascade Distillery died the death of Prohibition and was eventually reborn as the Cascade Hollow Distillery. The distillery moved from Cascade Hollow to Louisville, then to Frankfort (both in Kentucky) and then back to Cascade Hollow again. In the process, Cascade Tennessee Whisky became George Dickel Tennessee Whisky.

Cascade Hollow Distillery Operations

The operation at the Cascade Hollow Distillery is small by industry standards which allows for a personal and closely supervised operation. Since few of the grains necessary for making whiskey are grown locally in Tennessee, most of them are now shipped in—the corn from the Midwest and the rye and the barley from North and South Dakota. The same formula is used for both George Dickel products, No. 8 and No. 12. Although the exact percentages of the different grains is not known publicly, Dave Backus, the current Distillery Manager, points to the smaller percentage of rye used by George Dickel as a significant factor in producing the more mellow and smoother flavor. The distillery is selective and insists upon ex-

The beer still at George Dickel

James Harris

ceptionally clean grain with a low moisture content. Since Cascade Hollow distillery produces an average of 5.5 gallons of whiskey per bushel of grain, which is above the industry average, it must be doing something right with the way in which it selects and handles its grain.

The fermentation runs on three- and four-day cycles in stainless steel fermenters. This is a sour-mash operation with a 'set back' which exceeds 25 percent from the previous fermentations. The corn is cooked at 212 degrees Fahrenheit for 20–30 minutes before the mash is lowered to 180 degrees Fahrenheit for the addition of the rye. Finally, the mash is lowered to 145 degrees Fahrenheit, and the malted barley is added. No pressure cooking is used. The whiskey is 110 proof when it exits the Vendome beer still and 130 proof when it exits the doubler. It is reduced to 110 proof before entering the barrels for aging.

The special charcoal mellowing (or leeching) process distinctive of Tennessee Whiskey, which started with the original Lincoln County Process, receives special attention at Dickel. The stainless steel, charcoal mellowing tanks are filled to a depth of 10–12 feet with maple charcoal, with two special stainless plates and virgin wool blankets spaced at intervals down through the charcoal. The tanks are then flooded continuously with the new white dog, fresh from the doubler, which has been chilled to 40 degrees Fahrenheit. It takes as much as five to seven days for the whiskey to pass through the 12 feet of charcoal, but once the process is up and running there is a continuous flow of whiskey through the mellowing tanks so there is little or nor extra time necessary for this special mellowing step. The charcoal from the tanks is changed regularly to guarantee uniformity of quality.

Aging

Aging is another part of the process which receives special attention. According to Dave Backus, "You can't make a bad whiskey good during aging, but you can certainly make a good whiskey bad." Consequently, if a distillery produces a good whiskey, it makes good sense to do the aging properly so that the quality of the whiskey is not adversely affected during aging. There are eleven warehouses at the Cascade Hollow Distillery with a total capacity of 150,000 barrels. The warehouses have forced air ventilation and are heated in the winter. Unlike most American whiskey warehouses, the warehouses at Cascade Hollow are only one storey high. This prevents the wide fluctuations in aging conditions experienced in tall, multi-storey warehouses; hence it is not necessary to rotate the barrels to maintain even aging between barrels. Tasters regularly check as many as five different production dates at a time to compare and detect any variations in daily production runs. Although there are no ages indicated for George Dickel, no whiskey is bottled at less than five years, and most of it is seven or eight years old when bottled.

After the barrels are dumped, the whiskey is shipped in bulk to the Glenmore plant, one of the United Distillers facilities in Owensboro, Kentucky, to be bottled. There the whiskey undergoes another chill-filtering and demineralizing process to remove whatever calcium the whiskey might have picked up during the aging process. To our knowledge, George Dickel is the only whiskey made in the United States which undergoes two separate chill-filterings before being bottled.

'There Ain't Nothing Better'

'There ain't Nothing Better' is supposed to have been the slogan which George A. Dickel used to describe the original Cascade 'Tennessee Whisky,' but it is impossible to determine exactly when this expression was first used. Although Dickel does not list its citations on its labels as Jack Daniel's does, it has quite a few to its credit. Only recently entering tasting competitions, George Dickel won a bronze medal at the 1992 International Mercury Awards Competition. It won a Gold Medal in the 1993 Monde Selection Competitions, and most recently, George Dickel was named Tennessee category champion at the 1994 World Spirits Championship.

The original Cascade Distillery site in Cascade Hollow has recently been added to the National Register of Historic Places—a distinction shared only by Jack Daniel's and by Maker's Mark in Kentucky. Although there are currently no provisions for visitors to get to the site of the original Cascade Distillery, we believe that United Distillers may well preserve the area so that it is made suitable for visitors.

George Dickel Tennessee Whisky

The Cascade Hollow Distillery now produces three George Dickel labels. The oldest and best established of these are the No. 8, with a black label, and the No. 12 with a white label. The labels on these two whiskeys are interesting in several respects. First, the designations of 'No. 8' and 'No. 12' have nothing to do with age. The No. 8 is not eight years old, and the No. 12 is not twelve years old although, according to David Backus, the current distillery manager, the No. 12 is slightly older than the No. 8. The labels might lead a customer to think that there is a greater difference between these two whiskeys than there actually is. The black label on the No. 8 describes it as "Tennessee Sour Mash Whisky" while the label on the No. 12 describes it as the "original Tennessee Whisky." Both bottlings are of the same whiskey made from a single formula, and, of course, all of the whiskey made at the Cascade Hollow Distillery is sour mash whiskey. The main difference between the No. 8 and the No. 12 is the proof at which they are bottled. The No. 8 is bottled at 40 percent alcohol (80 proof), while the No. 12 is bottled at 45 percent alcohol (90 proof).

Dickel has also recently begun bottling the Special Barrel Reserve. This is a small-batch bottling on a really small scale. The first bottling, we understand, involved the dumping of only 70 barrels. The Special Barrel Reserve is a product of the same formula which produces George Dickel No. 8 and No. 12, but it is a much older and more mature whiskey, personally selected from the warehouses by Dave Backus. This is a ten-year-old whiskey and is bottled at 86 proof. Special Barrel Reserve is, to our knowledge, the oldest Tennessee Whiskey available.

Miss Annie's General Store

The General Store was recreated in 1958 when the new distillery was built and comes complete with an official United States Post Office. The General Store retains much of the appearance and atmosphere of a turn-of-the-century country store, complete with many of the brand name items which might have been found in such a store 90 or 100 years ago. There are various different George Dickel souvenirs for sale—everything from a Dickel barbecue apron to a brass Dickel Zippo lighter or a Dickel license plate—as well as an assortment of various country jams and other food items.

Visiting George Dickel

George Dickel and the Cascade Hollow Distillery welcomes visitors and is well-equipped to accommodate a large number of them comfortably. The visitors' center is located in Miss Annie's General Store (owned by the Distillery), which is located just across the road from the distillery. Guided tours are offered regularly Monday through Friday from 9:00 A.M. to 3:00 P.M. The people at George Dickel are extremely friendly and hospitable, and we recommend a visit very highly. To reach the distillery, from I-24 take Exit 25 and travel south on US 41 and then turn right (south) onto Tennessee State Route 4291 (Blanton Chapel Road). Go through Blanton Chapel to Ward Chapel, around Lake Normandy, and follow the signs to the distillery. From Tullahoma, go north on US ALT 41 to Tennessee State Route 269 and take a right (north) towards Normandy, and watch for signs to the distillery. As a result of a recent act of the Tennessee State Legislature, it is now possible to buy a special souvenir bottle of George Dickel when visiting the distillery which is the new bottling of the George Dickel Special Barrel Reserve—a ten-year-old, 86 proof Tennessee Whiskey.

TASTING NOTES

George Dickel No. 8, 40 percent and the No. 12, 45 percent

Very clean, smooth, light-bodied whiskies. We find the No. 12 to be a bit fuller in body. Perhaps because of their lighter bodies, the caramel and vanilla tones from the oak of the barrels are more distinctive in both of these whiskies than is found in most other whiskies. These are also extraordinarily smooth whiskies—a result of several factors: a formula which uses a low percentage of rye, the special charcoal filtering process, and the *two* chill filterings which all George Dickel whiskies receive. The bouquet and flavor of the George Dickel No. 8 are light, and while the bouquet and flavor of the No. 12 are a bit more full, neither of these whiskies is rich and robust in comparison with some Kentucky Bourbons. Perhaps some of the robust complexity of flavor has been traded for the exceptional smoothness. The finish of both the No. 8 and the No. 12 is quite smooth and lingering. We find that chilling either of these Dickel whiskies by adding ice or using them in mixes significantly reduces the already delicate flavor. We therefore recommend taking your Dickel neat, making it a real Tennessee sippin' whiskey.

Special Barrel Reserve, 43 percent, ten years

This is a small-batch whiskey which is personally selected by Dave Backus, and, so far as we know, is the oldest Tennessee Whiskey available. When we first heard of the Special Barrel Reserve, we were initially skeptical because, in our experience, Tennessee and Kentucky Whiskeys do not benefit from being in the barrel for long. Past a certain age the whiskey takes on a distinctively woody character in both bouquet and flavor. Whereas it is not unusual to find exceptional Scotch whiskies aged twelve, 15, or even 25 years, American whiskeys seem to reach the point of diminishing returns with aging somewhere around eight years. This is primarily because most Scotch is aged in either *used* sherry casks or *used* Bourbon barrels while Bourbon and Tennessee whiskey are both aged in *new,* charred oak barrels.

Our concerns were unfounded however. The Special Barrel Reserve has indeed benefitted from the extra time in the wood. Although still lighter in flavor and body than the most robust Kentucky Bourbons, the Special Barrel Reserve has taken on a more full-flavored character, both in bouquet and flavor, than either the No. 8 or the No. 12. While retaining the distinctive characteristics of Tennessee Whiskey, the Special Barrel Reserve has a greater complexity from the additional caramel and vanilla tones from the wood. This is an extraordinarily smooth whiskey with a long, lingering finish. Like the No. 8 and No. 12, the Special Barrel Reserve should be enjoyed neat, without ice or mixes. Our only complaint about the Special Barrel Reserve concerns its packaging. This whiskey is a member of the Bourbon Heritage Collection produced by United Distillers, and "Bourbon Heritage Collection" is displayed prominently on the box and the bottle. It is likely to be confusing to many customers to find such an excellent Tennessee Whiskey counted as part of a *Bourbon* collection.

5

Entertaining
with
Whiskey

If you are a serious whiskey enthusiast, you will undoubtedly focus your experiences with American whiskey on whiskey and ice, whiskey and pure water, or just plain whiskey. But it remains true that Bourbon and Tennessee whiskeys are remarkably adaptable—far more so than their Scottish and Irish cousins. This is most probably because of the characteristic vanilla-caramel sweet tones imparted by the new, charred oak barrels. For whatever reason, Bourbon and Tennessee whiskeys work well in a wide variety of cocktails, and are the foundation of several classic punches. These whiskeys are also remarkably useful in cooking, from hors d'oeuvres to desserts.

Whiskey Tastings

Wine enthusiasts have long made wine-tastings a familiar part of the social scenery. Especially since we are now finding more, higher-quality American whiskeys available than ever before, we feel that the times are right for whiskey tastings. The Jim Beam folks have tried to encourage this through their 'Bourbon Circle,' and Bourbon tastings show up with some frequency in the newspapers and magazines of Kentucky. They are quite easy to put together, so you might consider organizing a tasting for friends in your own home. There are a few simple rules to help make a whiskey tasting fun, educational, and safe.

1. To educate your guests (and yourself!) most effectively, keep the number of different whiskeys you taste in any one evening relatively small. Our experience suggests that five is a pretty good number.

2. Think about what you want your guests to learn. Answering this question will help you choose your whiskeys. For example, do you want to illustrate the variety that one can find in whiskeys? If so, you will want to choose whiskeys that show great contrasts. Perhaps you will choose: one to show the Beam style (Booker's, Baker's, Jim Beam); a Wild Turkey to illustrate a heavy, but less sweet whiskey; Maker's Mark to illustrate a light Bourbon style; Blanton's to highlight the sweet end of the spectrum; and Jack Daniel's or George Dickel to show how the Tennessee style differs from Bourbon.

    On the other hand, you might want to make a point about price. Certainly some of the high-price, 'boutique' whiskeys do offer something special. But do they all offer enough special taste to justify their cost?

    Or, finally, you may wish to challenge some prejudices and brand name loyalties. A *blind* tasting can yield surprising results.

3. Structure the tasting. It will help your guests if you, as host, help by guiding them through the tasting. Give your guests some sense of what to look for. Color is certainly far from being an important evaluative component, but starting there can help focus people's attention on the whiskey at hand. Direct them next to the 'nose,' the aroma. How would they describe the aroma—think in terms of both qualities and intensity? Next turn to the taste. Is it light-bodied, medium, or heavy? Does it roll around and fill the mouth, or does it affect

only certain parts? Is it sharp or mellow, rough or smooth? Is it simple, one dimensional, or is it complex? How would they describe the finish? Long or short? Pleasant or not? Is the finish different from the initial taste?

Encourage your guests to jot down their reactions to each whiskey, including not only adjectives, but also some evaluative descriptions.

4. Tasting and inebriation do not go together. Along those lines, time your tasting so that it happens near the beginning of your guests' stay. Don't do your tasting after dinner and dessert, just before your guests will be hopping into car to drive home!

5. Enjoy yourselves. If you are going to have guests over to enjoy some whiskey, consider highlighting whiskey in the foods you offer them. To give you a few ideas of what you might do, we include the following recipes, including a few cocktail and punch recipes you might wish to explore.

Cocktails, Punches, Coffee

The possibilities for American whiskey-based drinks are nearly endless. The sweetness and mellowness of a good Bourbon or Tennessee whiskey make for a drink that can stand by itself or be incorporated in a cocktail or punch mixture. Any good bar book will have numerous recipes, but we can't help but offer a few classics here.

MINT JULEP

The mint julep must be the best-known whiskey drink in America. With its icy chill and its fresh mint bouquet, it is ideally suited for those hot, humid, Southern summers. But don't let its summer associations put you off the julep just because it might not be summertime—just turn up the thermostat and stir up a glass! We offer two mint julep recipes for your consideration.

MINT JULEP:
THE BOOKER AND ANNIS NOE RECIPE

Make a simple syrup by boiling 2 cups of sugar and 2 cups of water for 5 minutes without stirring. Fill a jar loosely with sprigs of fresh mint, cover with cooled syrup. Cover and refrigerate 12 to 24 hours. Discard mint. Fill frosted julep glass with freshly crushed ice, pour in 1 tablespoon of mint syrup and 2 ounces of Jim Beam Bourbon Garnish with a sprig of mint and serve at once.

MINT JULEP: THE JACK DANIEL'S VERSION

Jack Daniel's: The Spirit of Tennessee Cookbook (by Lynne Tolley and Pat Mitchamore) offers four versions of juleps. But we thought this particular version, called "A Superior Mint Julep," most worthy of mention here.

> INGREDIENTS:
> *1 teaspoon sugar*
> *2 teaspoons water*
> *3 sprigs fresh mint*
> *3 ounces Jack Daniel's Whiskey*

Use a chilled 10-ounce glass. Throw away the sugar, water and the mint. Pour the Jack Daniel's Whiskey over ice. Makes 1 serving.

MANHATTAN

This is an easy drink to make and a very pleasant one to drink. Use a good, rich Bourbon, call it a Bourbon Manhattan, and the results will be great.

> *2 ounces Bourbon*
> *1/2 ounce sweet vermouth*
> *dash of bitters*

Stir with ice in a mixing glass. Strain into a cocktail glass and garnish with a cherry.

WHISKEY SOUR

2 ounces of whiskey
1 ounce lemon juice
$^1/_2$ to 1 teaspoon powdered sugar

Shake vigorously with ice. Strain into a glass. The traditional garnish is an orange slice with a cherry speared to it.

OLD FASHIONED

In a glass, muddle:

$^1/_2$ teaspoon sugar
splash of water
dash of bitters

Add ice and stir in 1–2 ounces whiskey.
Garnish with a cherry, a slice of orange, or preferably both.

WHISKEY PUNCH

This is a reliable favorite at the Waymack house, and has become known among his graduate students as 'Waymack's Truth Punch.'

2 bottles of whiskey
4 ounces lemon juice
4 ounces lime juice
1 can of frozen orange juice (12 ounces) partially thawed
2 cups pineapple juice
1 liter of ginger ale

Stir all but the ginger ale in a punch bowl with an ice block. Just before serving, gently add the ginger ale. Garnish with orange slices and a few cherries.

We prefer to use one of the more 'gingery' ginger ales, rather than the blander ones. If possible, it helps to chill everything before mixing the punch. Finally, as mixed this is a fairly strong punch: if you expect your guests to be particularly thirsty, or if you're worried that the punch might elicit more truths than desirable, you can cut back on the proportion of whiskey by up to one third.

KENTUCKY MULLED CIDER

For the colder months, this warm drink, from *That Special Touch,* a cookbook by Sandra Davis, highlighting Maker's Mark Bourbon, is a real gem.

> *1 cup Maker's Mark*
> *4 cups cider*
> *1 lemon, thinly sliced*
> *6 cloves*
> *$1/2$ tsp. allspice*
> *2 sticks cinnamon*

Combine all the ingredients. Heat to boiling point and serve. Serves about three.

DICKEL HOT TODDY

This cold-weather drink comes with the compliments of the folks at George Dickel.

> *1 teaspoon fine grain sugar*
> *2 cloves*
> *Slice of lemon*
> *Piece of cinnamon stick*
> *2 ounces George Dickel Tennessee Whisky*

Combine all in an old-fashioned glass or mug. Add $1^1/2$ ounces (or a little more) boiling water. Stir.

AMERICAN COFFEE

We all have heard of Irish Coffee. Well, Bourbon and Tennessee Whiskey make a coffee that is at least as good, perhaps better. Simply take a cup of hot coffee (about 5 to 6 ounces). Add $1^1/2$ ounces American whiskey and 1 rounded teaspoon sugar. Stir. Then top with lightly sweetened whipped cream.

Hors d'oeuvres and Appetizers

BOURBON SAUSAGE BITES

From the recipe files of Booker and Annis Noe, we have this delightful finger food.

> *1 pound fresh pork sausage or Italian sausage removed*
> *   from casing*
> *2 cups aged cheddar cheese, grated*
> *2 cups buttermilk biscuit mix*
> *4 Tablespoons Jim Beam Bourbon*
> *2 teaspoons minced fresh sage, or*
> *1 teaspoon dried*
> *2 teaspoons minced fresh Italian parsley*
> *2 Tablespoons minced shallots or scallions*
> *salt and pepper to taste*

1. Preheat oven to 400 degrees Fahrenheit

2. Combine sausage, cheese, baking mix and Jim Beam Bourbon in a mixing bowl and mix well.

3. Add remaining ingredients and blend well.

4. Form walnut-sized balls and place on rack on cooking sheet so that sausage fat drains off.

5. Bake at 400 degrees Fahrenheit for 20 minutes until golden brown.

   Remove from rack immediately and serve.
   Makes about 60 pieces.

'SPIRIT OF KENTUCKY' CHEESE BALL

This easy but rewarding recipe comes from *That Special Touch,* by Sandra Davis.

> *1 pound butter, softened*
> *1 pound Roquefort or bleu cheese*
> *¹/₂ cup Maker's Mark*
> *¹/₄ cup sesame seeds*

Cream butter and cheese with sesame seeds. Add Bourbon slowly. Shape into a ball. Refrigerate for 24 hours. Serve with crackers or beaten biscuits.

Main Courses

WHISKEY MARINATED STEAK

We have had different versions of this at several restaurants. This recipe represents our straightforward interpretation.

> *4 quality steaks (we prefer New York strip)*
> *2 cups American whiskey*
> *2 cloves garlic, crushed*
> *¹/₄ cup Worcestershire sauce*
> *1 Tablespoon light brown sugar*
> *2 Tablespoons black peppercorns, crushed or coarsely*
>   *ground*

Combine all ingredients in a resealable plastic bag and marinate the steaks in the refrigerator for 3 to 8 hours, according to taste. Drain. Salt and pepper the steaks and grill over a fire. (We like to add a few wood chips to the fire for some smoke.)

AFTERNOON STEW

Another one of the many recipes that we have enjoyed from Sandra Davis's *That Special Touch,* this is just the thing for a cold day.

> *2 pounds beef stew meat*
> *1 can mushrooms*
> *³/₄ cup water*
> *¹/₄ cup Maker's Mark Bourbon*
> *1 can mushroom soup*
> *1 envelope dry onion soup mix*

Preheat oven to 325 degrees Fahrenheit. Mix all ingredients in casserole; cover. Bake in 325 degree oven for 3 hours. Serve with freshly baked biscuits.

EVAN WILLIAMS BOURBONGNON DE BOEUF

This recipe, from our friends at Heaven Hill, earned a 'Grand Champion' award at the Kentucky State Fair.

> *3–14¹/₂ oz. cans beef stock*
> *2 large yellow onions, chopped w/peel*
> *3 large carrots, broken into pieces*
> *4 ribs celery, w/leaves, broken*
>   *into pieces*
> *6 slices bacon*
> *boiling water*
> *3 lbs. stewing beef*
> *olive oil*
> *1 C. Evan Williams Bourbon*
> *2 Tbs. tomato paste*
> *3 cloves garlic minced*
> *1 tsp. fresh thyme leaves*
> *1 bay leaf*
> *salt (optional)*
> *1 lb. mushrooms, browned in butter*
> *24 pearl onions, browned in butter*
> *roux (¹/₂ C. flour browned in ¹/₂ C. butter)*

Night before serving, bring beef stock, yellow onions, celery, and carrots to a boil, then reduce heat and simmer for two hours. Cool. Strain the stock, discarding the vegetables, and refrigerate.

Next morning, chop the bacon into small pieces, then blanch with boiling water to cover. Drain off water and fry gently without burning. Remove the bacon, add olive oil when necessary, and brown the beef quickly on all sides. Remove the beef and deglaze the pan by heating and adding the bourbon. Cook it down until the volume is reduced by half.

Place in a crock pot the beef, bacon, stock, tomato paste, garlic, thyme, bay leaf and salt to taste. Cook on high for one hour, then reduce heat to low and continue to cook for four or five hours, or until the beef is very tender. Add the sauteed onions and mushrooms and cook for another 20 minutes. Thicken with the roux.

Side Dishes

YUMMY GEORGE DICKEL YAMS

There are numerous recipes for yams or sweet potatoes with whiskey included. We particularly like this one because of its orange flavors, as well as because of its charming presentation in orange cups.

> *4 lbs. sweet potatoes*
> *1 stick softened margarine*
> *$^1/_3$ cup George Dickel Whisky*
> *$^1/_3$ cup orange juice*
> *$^1/_2$ cup brown sugar*
> *$^3/_4$ tsp. salt*
> *$^1/_2$ tsp. cinnamon*
> *$^1/_3$ cup chopped pecans (optional)*
> *6 medium oranges made into orange cups**

Cook unpeeled yams in boiling salted water. Drain, cool and peel.

Mash the potatoes and add margarine, whiskey, orange juice, sugar, salt and cinnamon. Beat together until fluffy. Spoon pota-

---

* To make orange cups, slice 1/4 inch off the top of an orange. Spoon out orange flesh, leaving only the rind of the orange, forming a bowl. Rinse well.

toes into orange cups, sprinkling with nuts if desired. Bake 30 minutes at 350 degrees.

BOURBON BAKED BEANS

2 cans of baked beans
one small onion, finely diced
¹/₂ cup catsup
¹/₄ cup Bourbon
¹/₄ cup Worcestershire sauce
¹/₂ teaspoon liquid smoke
1¹/₂ Tablespoons brown sugar
1 teaspoon chili powder

Combine all ingredients. Bake at 350 degrees for 40–45 minutes.

Desserts

There is no shortage of desserts that make good use of whiskey.

KENTUCKY HIGH DAY PIE

From the kitchen of Ann Waymack, a classic Bourbon pie.

2 eggs
¹/₂ cup butter, melted
4 Tablespoons Bourbon
¹/₄ cup cornstarch
1 cup finely chopped pecans
1 cup (6 oz.) chocolate chips
1 unbaked pie shell

Preheat oven to 350 degrees Fahrenheit. In a large mixing bowl, beat the eggs. Gradually add the sugar, then add the Bourbon, and finally the butter. Blend in the cornstarch. Stir in the pecans and chocolate chips. Pour into the pie shell. Bake for 45–50 minutes.

Cool for one hour. Serve with whipped cream.

BOURBON BALLS

There are endless versions of this easy and very popular confection.

> *2 cups fine vanilla wafer crumbs*
> *1 cup finely chopped pecans*
> *1 cup confectioners' sugar, plus additional confectioners'*
>   *sugar for rolling*
> *2 Tablespoons cocoa*
> *2 Tablespoons light corn syrup*
> *¹/₃ cup Bourbon*

Mix all ingredients together. One at a time, take a teaspoonful of mixture, roll it into a ball, and roll the ball in the additional confectioners' sugar. Store in a tightly closed container.

GEORGE DICKEL'S APPLE CRISP

An excellent apple crisp from Dickel.

> *8 medium tart apples (Jonathan or Granny Smith)*
> *¹/₂ cup granulated sugar*
> *¹/₄ cup George Dickel Whisky*
> *³/₄ cup raisins*
> *¹/₂ cup chopped nuts (pecans or walnuts)*
> *³/₄ cup brown sugar (packed)*
> *¹/₂ cup flour*
> *³/₄ cup rolled oats*
> *1¹/₂ tsp. cinnamon*
> *¹/₂ cup soft butter*

Preheat oven to 375 degrees. Peel, core and slice apples. Toss with sugar, whisky, raisins and nuts. Place in 1¹/₂ quart buttered baking dish.

Blend together brown sugar, flour, rolled oats, cinnamon and butter. Spread mixture over apples. Bake 35 to 40 minutes until apples are tender and topping is golden brown. Serve warm topped with vanilla ice cream.

Serves 6 to 8

ROBERT E. LEE CAKE

This is an incredibly rich, and incredibly delectable cake, from United Distillers, the makers of Rebel Yell.

> *10 eggs, separated*
> *1 teaspoon lemon juice*
> *1 teaspoon orange juice*
> *1 teaspoon Rebel Yell*
> *2 cups cake flour*
> *¹/4 teaspoon salt*
> *2 cups sugar*

Beat egg yolks until lemon-colored. Add sugar, fruit juices, Rebel Yell. Beat egg whites until stiff, and fold into this mixture. Add sifted flour and salt. Bake in four greased and floured 8-inch round layer cake pans at 350 degrees for 20–30 minutes.

> *Frosting:*
>
> *3 cups sugar*
> *3 stiffly beaten egg whites*
> *1 teaspoon Rebel Yell*
> *1 cup water*
> *1 Tablespoon lemon juice*
> *1 cup grated coconut*

Boil sugar and water until it forms a soft ball. Pour over egg whites, beating constantly. Add lemon juice and Rebel Yell. Spread between layers, on top and sides of cake. Sprinkle coconut on top.

Bibliography

Carr, Jess. *The Second Oldest Profession: An Informal History of Moonshining in America.* Englewood Cliffs, NJ: Prentice-Hall, 1972.

Carson, Gerald. *The Social History of Bourbon: An Unhurried Account of Our Star-Spangled American Drink.* Lexington: University of Kentucky Press, 1963.

Crowgey, Henry G. *Kentucky Bourbon: The Early Years of Whiskeymaking.* Lexington: University of Kentucky Press, 1971.

Dabney, Joseph Earl. *Mountain Spirits: A Chronicle of Corn Whiskey from King James's Ulster Plantations to America's Appalachians and the Moonshine Life.* New York: Charles Scribner's Sons, 1974.

Davis, Sandra. *That Special Touch.* Springfield, KY: Special Touch, 1990. To order, call 1-800-393-8368.

Dick, Everett. *The Dixie Frontier.* New York: Capricorn Books, 1948.

Downard, William L. *Dictionary of the History of the American Brewing and Distilling Industries.* London: Greenwood Press, 1980.

Dykeman, Wilma. *Tennessee.* New York: Norton, 1975.

Farmer, Robert Crosbie. *Industrial and Power Alcohol.* London: Pittman, 1921.

Garrett, William Robertson and Albert Virgil Goodpasture. *History of Tennessee.* Nashville: Brandon, 1903.

Getz, Oscar. *Pictorial History of Whiskey.* Bardstown, KY: Barton Museum of Whiskey, 1975.

Getz, Oscar. *Whiskey: An American Pictorial History.* New York. McKay, 1978.

Giles, Janice Holt. *The Kentuckians.* Lexington: University of Kentucky Press, 1953.

The Goodspeed Histories of Giles, Lincoln, Franklin and Moore Counties of Tennessee. Columbia, TN: Woodward & Stinson. Printing Co., 1886.

Green, Ben A. *Jack Daniel's Legacy.* Shelbyville, TN: Ben A. Green, 1967.

Grossman, Harold J. (Revised by Harriet Lembeck) *Grossman's Guide to Wines, Beers, and Spirits.* New York: Charles Scribner's Sons, 1940.

Jackson, Michael. *The World Guide to Whisky.* Philadelphia: Running Press, 1987.

McWhiney Grady. *Cracker Culture: Celtic Ways in the Old South.* Tuscaloosa: University of Alabama Press, 1988.

Rorabaugh, W.J. *The Alcoholic Republic: An American Tradition.* Oxford: Oxford University Press, 1979.

Slaughter, Thomas. *The Whiskey Rebellion: Frontier Epilogue to the American Revolution.* Oxford: Oxford University Press, 1980.

Smith, Daniel. *A Short Description of the State of Tennassee* [sic]. Philadelphia: Lang and Ustick, 1796.

Tolley, L. and P. Mitchamore. *Jack Daniel's The Spirit of Tennessee Cookbook.* Nashville, TN: Rutledge Hill Press, 1988.

Wilkie, H.F. *Beverage Spirits in America: A Brief History.* New York: The Newcomen Society of England, 1947.

Index